YEAR GROUP
PHOTOCOPIABLES

YEAR

4

Paul and Jean Noble

CREDITS

Authors
Paul and Jean Noble

Editor
Dulcie Booth

Assistant Editor
David Sandford

Series Designer
Lynne Joesbury

Designer
Rachel Warner

Illustrations
Sarah Warburton

Cover photographs
Manipulated images © PHOTODISC (globe, dice, magnet, paint brush, disk),
© DIGITAL VISION (hand), © STOCKBYTE (mask).

Published by Scholastic Ltd,
Villiers House,
Clarendon Avenue,
Leamington Spa,
Warwickshire
CV32 5PR
Printed by Bell & Bain Ltd, Glasgow
Text © 2003 Paul and Jean Noble
© 2003 Scholastic Ltd
3 4 5 6 7 8 9 0   5 6 7 8 9 0 1 2

Visit our website at www.scholastic.co.uk

British Library Cataloguing-in-Publication Data
A catalogue record for this book is available from
the British Library.

ISBN 0-439-98302-9

CONTENTS

ACKNOWLEDGEMENTS

Material from the National Curriculum © Crown copyright. Reproduced with permission of the Controller of HMSO and the Queen's Printer for Scotland. Material from Programmes of Study in the National Curriculum © Qualifications and Curriculum Authority. Reproduced under the terms of HMSO Guidance Note 8. Material from the National Literacy Strategy *Framework for Teaching* and the National Numeracy Strategy *Framework for Teaching Mathematics* © Crown copyright. Reproduced under the terms of the HMSO Guidance Note 8.

Ordnance Survey for the use of map symbols, a section of the OS Landranger Map 121 and a section of the OS Landranger Map 164 © Crown Copyright. Reproduced with permission of Her Majesty's Stationery Office. Licence No. 100014536.

Stainer and Bell Ltd for the use of 'A Christmas carol' by Sydney Carter © Stainer and Bell Ltd (Galliard).

INTRODUCTION

Of all the teaching aids produced in the last 50 years, the worksheet has proved to be the most useful, the most flexible, the easiest to use, the cheapest, and often the most effective. But worksheets, like teachers, do not operate in a vacuum, for learning is a complex process that only works if there is intellectual activity. The learner's brain has to be switched on. It is up to you to capture their interest.

This book offers considerable support to teachers working under many pressures, not least that of time constraint, but none of its contents will do the teaching for you. You still have to engage the learner's mind, stimulate interest in the subject and, more often than not, set the context for the work. That said, we are sure that you will find much to help you here and plenty that will challenge, amuse and satisfy your children. The *Year Group Photocopiables* series draws on substantial teaching experience and provides a readily accessible classroom support, particularly when you are limited by time or challenged by voracious learners. Supply teachers and others 'caught on the hop' will also be able to rely on this material to help them cope with demanding days.

Teaching Year 4

Year 4 has been called the 'drifter's year' because, as OFSTED have observed, it is the year when the progress witnessed in the previous year is not always maintained, when the impetus to move on somehow seems to be lost. What is it that makes this difference? It is true that children do need time to absorb and

consolidate the enormous amount of learning that has already taken place, but children are still growing and changing and their learning should also progress. Perhaps the fact that Year 4 lacks the excitement and pressure that the years of change at the beginnings and ends of the key stages possess, has something to do with it. Moreover, there are no statutory assessments. If one examines the National Curriculum for Year 4, one can identify the phased repetition of some basic concepts, processes and skills. Nevertheless there is new subject matter to be tackled in every aspect of the curriculum so there is no reason why progress should splutter to a halt. Learning is as new and exciting as ever.

Because the National Curriculum, prescriptive though it is, still involves making choices, and because we cannot cover everything in a book such as this, we have relied heavily upon the Schemes of Work drawn up by the QCA to help us make our choices. These Schemes are acknowledged as the basis for many school syllabuses (see www.qca.org.uk or www.standards.dfes.gov.uk/schemes).

What the photocopiable sheets cover

This particular volume is based upon the range of curriculum subjects and experiences that are described within *The National Curriculum: Handbook for primary teachers in England* (www.nc.uk.net). Inevitably, weighting has been given to the core subjects (English, mathematics and science) and the worksheets have been compiled bearing in mind the demands of the Literacy and Numeracy Strategies as well as QCA subject guidance. The non-core foundation subjects (design and technology, information and communication technology, history, geography, art and design and music, with the exception of physical education) are included but in varying degrees, depending upon the suitability of the content to the photocopiable format. Non-foundation subjects such as religious education, PSHE and citizenship are covered where subject matter allows. The photocopiable sheets do not, of course, cover everything and they cannot constitute a complete curriculum. Rather like basic car insurance, the cover provided here is fundamental rather than comprehensive. A book that attempted to be comprehensive would be many times larger than this, as well as being difficult to justify in principle. Nobody would want Year 4 children to overdose on worksheets.

The choice of photocopiable sheets was made on the following grounds:

● Content and activities must translate sensibly into the photocopiable format. (Activities that are predominantly 'hands-on', colour dependent or oral have been largely avoided.)

● Activities must be worthwhile (in that they contribute towards achieving specific learning objectives) and interesting for the children.

● Subject matter should relate directly to the prescribed National Curriculum.

● Content should satisfy the demands of the Numeracy and Literacy strategies where possible.

We have largely avoided providing repetitious sheets in favour of range of cover and in order to keep the book to a manageable size. However, suggestions for reinforcement and extension are included in the teacher's notes.

Using the material

Before using one of the photocopiable sheets it is recommended that you read the teacher's notes that accompany it. These have been deliberately kept brief and contain four sections:

Objective

This states the learning objective(s). Every objective is linked to the curriculum guidance issued by the government – in English and mathematics, for example, the objectives match targets specified in the Numeracy and Literacy Strategies. Objectives have been stated in direct and non-pretentious terms. However, it is not claimed that children completing a particular sheet will therefore fully achieve that objective – we wish that teaching and learning were that easy.

What to do

This section provides notes on how the activity should be introduced and worked through with the children. These instructions repeatedly refer to the adult support that children will require and to the importance of talk and discussion. It is very important to get children to 'think out loud' as an aid to learning, but we have also made the assumption that children will be given oral instruction and support. Instructions given on the sheets are kept brief, although many children will now have reached a sufficient level of reading competency to cope with quite complex written instructions. Sometimes the text serves as a memory jogger to the teacher rather than as instruction to the child. The teacher's notes state when, and what, equipment will be required (usually very little), how the activity might be taught (whole class, group, individually), and the degree of teacher support that is likely to be needed.

Differentiation

This section covers many strategies for differentiation, including: **Modification:** we suggest that the sheet is changed in some way, instructions are omitted, language modified, or sections altered. **Material support:** help is suggested in the form of books, apparatus or equipment. **Co-operative support:** solo activities are changed into group or paired activities where children can support each other. **Adult support or intervention:** adults are required to supervise, interpret or help in some other appropriate way. **Time allocation:** it is suggested that children are given more time to complete a task or are given more of the teacher's time. **By outcome:** different expectations may be held for particular groups of children (for example, some might give oral rather than written answers).

When you have opted to use one of the sheets you will have made a judgement that the activity is appropriate to the abilities of most of the class. If it is too difficult for some, first question whether this activity should be given to those children at all: if there is a marked mismatch between ability and task, reject the task. (Perhaps a suitable activity will be found in an earlier volume in this series.) Where a task is too easy for a child, once again, you should first question the decision to use that sheet at all. In practice, an 'easy' task may be used as reinforcement of prior learning, but when a more able child completes such a task more rapidly and more accurately than the rest of the class, you should look to provide extra work to extend that child's learning.

Extension

Extension activities can be used as a form of differentiation for more able children but they are mainly intended to provide some form of reinforcement to help achieve the objective. Apart from where particular apparatus or teaching is required, most of the extension activities could be completed at home. It is recommended that the issues being dealt with (including the support provided for parents), the value of completing the work at home and competing demands on the child are all considered before homework is set.

Progression

The order of the photocopiable sheets has been kept as logical as possible – the activity on sheet one would usually be expected to be taught before sheet ten, for example. However, this order will not necessarily match the order of your teaching programme, and in some subject areas there is simply no obvious order for the teaching of particular activities. Nevertheless, a thread of progression runs through the book, and, more visibly, through the series. This is inevitable as the material is tied to a progressive National Curriculum. It does mean, however, that reference can be made, both forward and backward, for more or less challenging activities for the children to undertake.

ENGLISH

It is said that language is the gift that separates humans from the rest of the animal kingdom, a statement easy to agree with. After all, can you think of any human attribute or skill comparable, in its level of sophistication and complexity, to language? And of all the languages in the world, English is not the easiest to learn, or so one might surmise from observing foreign students trying to sort out 'reading' from 'Reading'. English has been analysed and dissected over and over again for the purposes of teaching and learning, but even so, getting to grips with the rules that govern it is difficult, partly because, like all living languages, English is constantly changing.

Just as the Literacy Strategy struggles to cover a comprehensive language programme at Year 4, we cannot expect to cover the strategy in a few worksheets. So we have not attempted to do so; instead we have adopted a sampling approach. We have aimed to cover a range of material and topics from the National Literacy Strategy for Year 4, choosing our subject matter by sticking to the guiding principle of concentrating on what lends itself most readily to the worksheet format. Fortunately this left us with a great deal of language work that could be tackled effectively, although you will find a distinct bias towards word- and sentence-level work and less emphasis on text-level work, where comprehension and composition really demand stimulus and experience not readily compressed into a sheet of A4. Perhaps more importantly, text-level work can also benefit greatly from adult intervention and social interaction.

Words containing 'k' (page 12)

Objective: To use visual skills to develop spelling, recognising common letter strings and critical features of words.

What to do: Following the instructions on the sheet should pose few problems but children will need decent dictionaries to undertake this task effectively. The additional words should be written in the appropriate part of the kipper. There are a number of letter combinations and patterns that the children might notice (such as *kn*, *ck*, *sk*). They could record these or, better still, report back their observations to a plenary session of the whole class.

Differentiation: It helps if children have suitable reference books that they can handle easily. Provide less able children with books containing clear, boldly printed collections of words.

Extension: Give children a blank fish and a new challenge of a similar sort, using a different letter.

Words ending in 'y' (page 13)

Objective: To examine what happens to words ending in *y* when changes are made and to notice patterns in the changes.

What to do: You may wish to discuss word patterns and spelling strategies before letting children work on this sheet. (Not least in the context *Does it look right?*) Encourage the children to add more words of their own to the lists. Explain the pattern for those that don't notice it – where there is a vowel before the final *y* the new word is made by simply adding *s*; where there is not, the *y* is replaced by *ies*.

Differentiation: Provide less able children with appropriate wordbanks and dictionaries.

Extension: Provide practice at spelling these words using the look–say–cover–write–check strategy.

One of our consonants is missing! (page 14)

Objectives: To identify misspelt words; to spell two-syllable words containing double consonants.

What to do: This exercise must emphasise the correct, not the incorrect, so get children to cross out the wrong spelling each time – felt-tipped obliteration is a good idea! In each case the middle consonant is doubled.

Differentiation: Spelling is not solely a visual skill and children need to write words, training their hands to learn common patterns. Extend (double) the number of practice attempts for those children who you feel need this reinforcement.

Extension: Get children to practise spelling these words (using the look–say–cover–write–check strategy). Ask them to make a further collection of words with double consonants in the middle. This would make a reasonable task for homework.

Adding 'ing' to verbs (page 15)

Objective: To spell regular verb endings (in this case *ing*).

What to do: Explain the sheet to the children before they begin. Each word in a rectangular box can be linked to a word enclosed in an oval (by drawing a pencil line). Linking the words should be easy, but you will need to explain the colour code that they have to use when shading in the pairs. *What happens when ing is added?*

Differentiation: Some children may find the task easier if the linked words are written down. Alternatively they can cut out the words and match them together. Even less able children should be expected to look for the spelling patterns.

Extension: Challenge children to write down what happens to (say) ten more verbs of their own choosing, when *ing* is added. *Which groups do they belong to?*

Tagged on the end: suffixes
(page 16)

Objective: To recognise and spell the suffixes *hood, al, ary, ship, ness*.

What to do: The vocabulary is quite demanding on this sheet and you may wish to go through the words first, checking that children understand their meanings. You can let children check their own work if they are competent at using dictionaries.

Differentiation: Provide dictionaries and wordbanks for less able children.

Extension: Challenge children to say what difference the suffix has made to the meaning of the original word. Get them to write out definitions of the new words. They can use a dictionary. This could be a homework task.

Finding adverbs (page 17)

Objective: To identify adverbs and recognise their function in a sentence.

What to do: These are open-ended questions that allow for a range of answers. You should give credit for use of the most appropriate and powerful words. Draw children's attention to the fact that many adverbs end in *ly*.

Differentiation: A thesaurus, suitably compiled for children, is ideal support for the less literate.

Extension: Make sure that children understand how adverbs qualify the meaning of verbs. Encourage them to use adverbs more frequently in their writing. Have a morning of 'adverb mania' where both you and the children have to qualify as many verbs as possible in your speech. 'Please, Miss, can I go to the lavatory, dramatically?' (It may be nonsense, but you get the idea.)

Homophones (page 18)

Objective: To distinguish between the spellings and meanings of common homophones.

What to do: Homophones sound the same but are spelt differently. Children select the correct homophones to make each sentence make sense and write it in the spaces provided.

Differentiation: Dictionaries will help less able children a little but they may gain more from the support of a partner if they work at this task co-operatively.

Extension: Ask children to collect homophones. Can they find, for example, ten new ones? This would make a good homework task.

The tense connection (page 19)

Objective: To understand that the tense of a verb can be changed.

What to do: Understanding of the word 'tense', as well as the ability to use it appropriately, is an important part of this activity. Make sure that the meaning is well established in the minds of the class. (Tense refers to time.) Get the children to carry out the task using a ruler and a pencil. They may use different colours for each collection of verbs. The last question on the sheet is open-ended and should be a matter for general discussion. This sheet is marked most speedily by visual reference.

Differentiation: Put less able children in pairs or small groups to do this task.

Extension: Give the children a list of words, some of which are verbs, and ask them to sort the verbs from the non-verbs by applying the 'tense test'. (One test of whether a word is a verb or not is that its tense can be changed.) This is a possible task for homework.

Belongs to... (page 20)

Objective: To use an apostrophe to mark possession accurately.

What to do: This sheet does squeeze in rather a lot about apostrophes, and if it is to be used in its complete form, it would be best to use it at the end of a period of teaching about the use of apostrophes. Alternatively you can divide the sheet up into three sections and use each section separately as and when you think fit. This is best marked by visual reference.

Differentiation: Limit teaching to one clear aspect of the topic at a time or the uncomprehending will scatter apostrophes like confetti.

Extension: Lots of practice is needed to establish these rules. Sharpen up children's awareness of the presence of apostrophes by getting them to record how many apostrophes they can spot in a piece of writing. Wrongly placed apostrophes are quite common in advertising and local newspapers. Ask children to keep a watchful eye for errors.

Its or it's? (page 21)

Objective: To distinguish between the use of the apostrophe for contraction and possession.

What to do: You will need to go over the principles involved here more than once before letting children loose on the task. The simple 'it is' replacement test should enable them to complete the ten sentences without error, so make sure that they understand this first.

Differentiation: Cut out a paper tab with 'it is' written on it. Let less confident children physically put this into each space and test whether it works by reading the new sentence out loud (this is best done in pairs). If it does, then they write 'it's' in the space. It is easier to do this if you enlarge the sheet.

Extension: Give plenty of practice by creating more cloze-procedure sentences.

Punctuation marks (page 22)

Objective: To identify common punctuation marks and to respond to them appropriately when reading.

What to do: Get children to work on this activity in pairs or in small groups. They can tally how many of each punctuation mark there are against the names at the top of the sheet. This is the sort of task that is best corrected and discussed in a whole-class session.

Differentiation: Mixed-ability grouping is the best solution to catering for less able children in this case.

Extension: Encourage children to use appropriate punctuation in their own writing. You could get them to focus on punctuation when next revising or editing their work.

Compound words (page 23)

Objectives: To investigate compound words; to recognise that identification of compound words can help spelling where pronunciation obscures it, such as *cupboard*.

What to do: The picture clues are not answers but simply intended to help children solve the puzzles. You could point this out by giving an example such as: *The first question shows 'cupboard' not mugbox, teablock, or handleslab*. The answers are: **1.** cupboard; **2.** handbag; **3.** football; **4.** toothbrush; **5.** honeymoon; **6.** gooseberry; **7.** buttercup; **8.** bulldog; **9.** drumstick; **10.** rainbow; **11.** nutcracker; **12.** pushchair; **13.** matchbox; **14.** sunflower; **15.** grapefruit; **16.** ladybird.

Differentiation: Provide dictionaries for less able children to check their answers for correct spelling.

Extension: Children can have fun inventing their own compound words, for example a pram becomes a 'babypusher'. Challenge them to invent four compound words of their own.

Poem parts (page 24)

Objective: To recognise and understand terms that identify specific parts of a poem.

What to do: Children will need decent dictionaries for this task. It is best marked visually or tackled in a group or class discussion. Read the whole poem to and with the children. Familiarity with poetry – reading it, having it read to them, browsing poetry books – is essential if children are to tackle this task with any hope of success.

Differentiation: Less able children should work with an adult and undertake the sheet as an oral exercise.

Extension: Read lots of poetry to the class on a regular basis. Ask children to choose a favourite poem and to be prepared to identify its constituent parts, as a possible homework task.

Points of view (page 25)

Objective: To present a point of view in writing, selecting and organising arguments to link them together effectively.

What to do: The sheet is self-explanatory, although you may wish to go through the arguments with the class before setting them to do the task. Most children should be able to write the letter effectively but you should have a session where the class can evaluate the letters. Which is the most important argument? Which points might be discarded? Which point should be made first? The answers are, of course, a matter of judgement and debate.

Differentiation: Let the less able cut out the statements and arrange them in order of importance. They then need only join the sentences together coherently.

Extension: Collect letters to the press, articles and other examples of arguments. Read them to the children and get them to evaluate their effectiveness.

Purr-suasion (page 26)

Objective: To evaluate adverts and to recognise how a product is presented, what strategies are used and so on.

What to do: Children could usefully tackle this assignment in small groups. You might find it useful to make an OHP transparency to use in class discussion. *How is this product being sold?* The advertisement uses humour, exaggerated claims, jingles, special offers, attention-grabbing strategies, scientific claims and so on. Get children to think about the appeal of this advertisement. How honest do they think it is?

Differentiation: As long as a group approach is adopted, differentiation will be by expectation and outcome.

Extension: Make a class collection of advertisements. Identify the elements used such as humour, puns, science and so on. This could be a homework task.

Making a new ending (page 27)

Objective: To write an alternative ending to a known story.

What to do: Children use the writing frames, and their imagination, to construct a new ending to the well-known story. They should focus on the ending only, so the task need not involve writing a lengthy script.

Differentiation: Use your established classroom strategies and teaching techniques for the support of poor writers (try cards, spelling books, wordbanks, adult assistance, and so on) to support less able children in this activity.

Extension: Class discussion should take place about the effect of some of the endings, especially how they might change our views of characters in the story. This discussion could lead on to a discussion of a well-known (suitable) TV programme, or book, in the same terms.

Writing up notes (page 28)

Objective: To fill out brief notes into connected prose.

What to do: Follow the instructions on the sheet. Look for connected and coherent prose, not just a cut-and-paste job.

Differentiation: Give help to those who have difficulty reading the phrases. Make it clear that as the report is written in the first person they should pretend to be the police officer writing the report.

Extension: Children could write the story as a play or TV script, which could then be acted out.

Edit this (page 29)

Objectives: To edit a story to fit a particular space; to edit down a passage by deleting the less important elements.

What to do: Read this (unfortunately) true story to the class first. Explain how it needs to be edited so that it tells the story succinctly. What unimportant bits could be left out?

Differentiation: Differentiate by making this a co-operative activity for some.

Extension: The finished 'edited' version needs to be written up in some way and tested on an audience to see if it still manages to convey the main events of the story. You might provide children with a word-processed version that they could edit on screen and print when complete.

A simile poem (page 30)

Objective: To understand the use of similes.

What to do: Explain what a *simile* is to the children. The first part should be relatively simple if the children look at the picture clues. The importance of the first part of the phrases needs to be stressed, as all of the similes are intended to describe either the man's exit from the room, or the old man's character and appearance.

Differentiation: This activity will be differentiated by imagination if anything and outcomes will vary according to children's creativity and word power.

Extension: Set the children the task of simile-spotting: *How many similes can you spot in your reading book?* Remember, *like* and *as* are the key words.

Groups of adjectives (page 31)

Objectives: To explore the nature of adjectives; to place them in order of intensity.

What to do: Following the instructions on the sheet, children first sort the words according to the categories given. They will need a thesaurus in order to complete the last two examples. This is only a first step in exploring the use of adjectives and, in this case, the extension task is essential if the learning objective is to be achieved.

Differentiation: Supervised group work is the preferred differentiation for the less able. An adult may be required to help with particular words.

Extension: Take the words in each list and ask children to sort them by degree or intensity. *Which is the most powerful? The least?* Reasonable answers (change in use makes definitive answers hard to establish) are: satisfied, content, pleased, happy; bitter, angry, mad, furious, livid, wild; cool, chilly, frosty, cold, freezing; unharmed, protected, safe, secure.

Placing adverbs (page 32)

Objective: To identify and use adverbs correctly in sentences.

What to do: This helps to establish in children's minds that not all adverbs end in *ly*. Follow the instructions on the sheet. The answers are open-ended.

Differentiation: One sentence from each section should be the minimum requirement for less able children. Challenge more able children to write a sentence with an adverb from each category, for example *The prince left his socks* everywhere, *but* later *the maid* carefully *put them away.*

Extension: Challenge children to find other adverbs that will fit into the categories on the sheet, a task that might be carried out for homework.

What would you have done?
(page 33)

Objective: To write independently, linking to their own experience, about situations that arise in stories.

What to do: The writing frames are intended to help children formulate coherent responses based upon their own feelings and experiences. They have to put themselves 'in the frame' as it were – *What would you have done if…?*

Differentiation: Talk is the best way of getting less confident children focused on this task. Divide into small groups, ideally with an adult, to direct the discussion. Children should formulate their responses orally in the first instance and then they can be given assistance in recording them as necessary.

Extension: The children could debate and/or rewrite stories from the news, from films, fiction or fact. Stories can be debated from their own viewpoint using similar writing frames to those used in this exercise.

Words containing 'k'

● Add some words of your own to each group. Use a dictionary.
● Do you notice any patterns in each group?

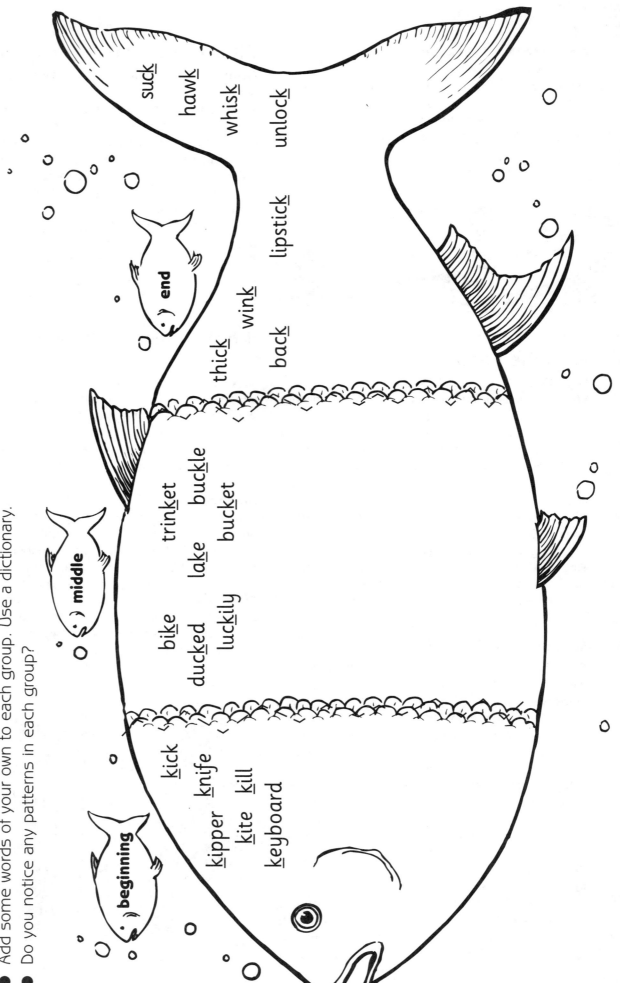

beginning

kick
kipper knife
kite kill
keyboard

middle

bike trinket buckle
ducked lake bucket
luckily

end

suck
hawk
whisk
unlock
lipstick
thick wink
back

Words ending in 'y'

● Use these words to make new words to fit in either list **A** or list **B**.

stray	fry	pray	carry
stay		play	hurry
try	empty	enjoy	cry

A

_____ s

_____ s

_____ s

_____ s

_____ s

_____ s

_____ s

_____ s

B

_____ ies

_____ ies

_____ ies

_____ ies

_____ ies

_____ ies

_____ ies

_____ ies

● Can you see a pattern in each list?
● Think of some more words to add to the lists.

One of our consonants is missing!

● You should be seeing double in these words but one of the consonants is missing.

● Which one? Spell the word correctly three times and remember the spelling. Cross out the wrongly spelt words!

~~puzle~~	→	puzzle	puzzle	puzzle
woble	→	_____	_____	_____
buton	→	_____	_____	_____
colar	→	_____	_____	_____
miten	→	_____	_____	_____
nible	→	_____	_____	_____
misile	→	_____	_____	_____
netle	→	_____	_____	_____
mesage	→	_____	_____	_____
jely	→	_____	_____	_____
geting	→	_____	_____	_____
hamer	→	_____	_____	_____
puting	→	_____	_____	_____
leson	→	_____	_____	_____
batle	→	_____	_____	_____

Adding 'ing' to verbs

- Link these words in pairs. The first one is done for you.
- If the last consonant is doubled, colour the pair in **red**.
- If the last 'e' is dropped, colour the pair in **yellow**.
- If there is no change, colour the pair in **blue**.

Tagged on the end: suffixes

● Use the suffixes **hood**, **al**, **ary**, **ship** and **ness** to make new words from this list.

critic _____   craftsman _____

neighbour _____   father _____

station _____   sad _____

member _____   cheerful _____

diction _____   second _____

fiction _____   leader _____

mother _____   herb _____

dictator _____   department _____

● Can you write any other words that have these suffixes?

Finding adverbs

Find five adverbs to finish each of these people's sentences. An example has been done for you in each speech bubble.

Well Gary, I think that the players passed the ball **accurately**.

In Wales the wind will blow **ferociously**.

I finished my homework **swiftly**.

MATHS

KEVIN ROGERS

_____

_____

_____

_____

_____

_____

_____

_____

_____

_____

_____

_____

_____

Homophones

Choose the correct word from the brackets to fill the gaps.

1. There are _____ green bottles hanging on the wall. What are they _____? (for, four)

2. There are _____ more green bottles in the fridge. I must go _____ the supermarket _____ get four more. You can come _____. (to, too, two)

3. Green bottles are all _____ selling, _____ shelves are full of them but _____ is another bottle shop in Bognor.
(their, there, they're)

4. How can I carry these bottles all the _____ home? They _____ too much. (weigh, way)

5. Can you _____ what I am saying? They only sell green bottles _____. (here, hear)

6. Bottles to the left, bottles to the _____ , there are bottles everywhere. I will _____ a letter to the manager and complain. (write, right)

7. A _____ shop in the High Street sells blue bottles. I _____ that someone would sell a different colour. (knew, new)

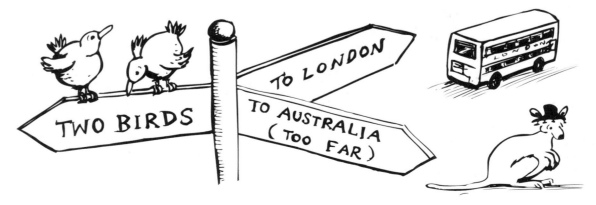

The tense connection

● Join the present tense verb to its past tense. You will find it inside the same shape.

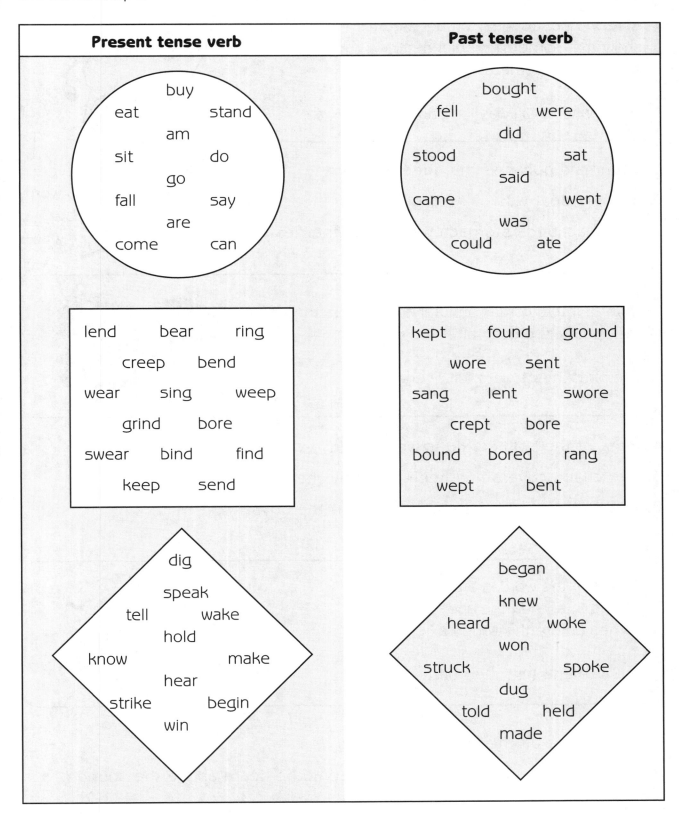

Present tense verb	Past tense verb

buy
eat   stand
am
sit   do
go
fall   say
are
come   can

bought
fell   were
did
stood   sat
said
came   went
was
could   ate

lend   bear   ring
creep   bend
wear   sing   weep
grind   bore
swear   bind   find
keep   send

kept   found   ground
wore   sent
sang   lent   swore
crept   bore
bound   bored   rang
wept   bent

dig
speak
tell   wake
hold
know   make
hear
strike   begin
win

began
knew
heard   woke
won
struck   spoke
dug
told   held
made

● Investigate the pairs of words.

Belongs to...

Follow the examples and add the apostrophes to the sentences.

Rule 1: Apostrophes can be used to show that something belongs to someone or something:

The donkey**'s** tail was long and furry.

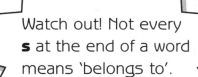

Watch out! Not every **s** at the end of a word means 'belongs to'.

1. The maid polished the queens crown.

2. Arthurs seat was painted green.

3. The blackbirds stomach was full of cherries.

Rule 2: If the word is a plural ending in **s**, then the apostrophe goes after the **s**:

The bird**s'** nests were full of eggs.

4. Most of the soldiers guns were clean.

5. The chairs covers had been faded by the sun.

6. The girls tongues were poking out at the boys.

Rule 3: If the word is a plural not ending in **s**, then the apostrophe comes before the added **s**:

The women**'s** hats blew off.

7. The cat ate all the childrens dinners.

8. During the song, the mens voices could be heard above the sound of the trumpets.

9. He cut off the sheeps tails with scissors.

Its or it's?

The donkey flapped **its** ears. → no apostrophe

It's raining. → apostrophe 's'

Use **its** or **it's** to fill the blanks in these sentences.

(REMEMBER if you can replace **its** with **it is** then it should be **it's**. If you can't then **its** is correct.)

1. Hamlet the cat chewed _____ tail.

2. Put your coats on children, _____ raining outside.

3. _____ a long way to Tipperary.

4. I think _____ the first time Swindon have been in the Cup Final.

5. Don't wear that tie with that shirt, _____ green.

6. The helicopter dipped _____ nose and then sped away.

7. _____ brown with crust around _____ edges. What is it?

8. In Grimsby _____ easy to buy fish and chips.

9. In Australia _____ easy to get sunburnt.

10. _____ Sunday and _____ raining. A bird shakes _____ wet

wings and flies to the highest branch of the tree.

Punctuation marks

● Punctuation helps a reader make sense of writing. Do you know these marks? Link them to their correct names.

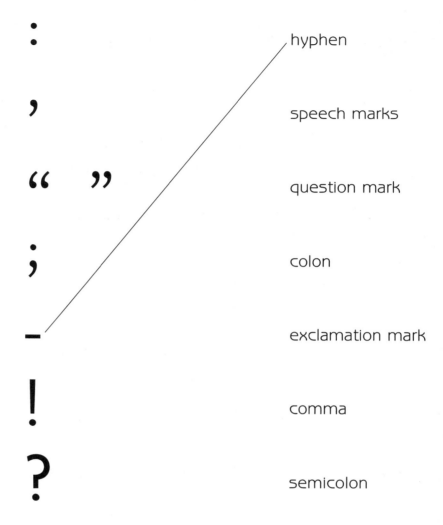

:

,

" "

;

–

!

?

hyphen

speech marks

question mark

colon

exclamation mark

comma

semicolon

● Underline all the punctuation marks in this writing. How many of each are there?

Tim has served an ace! Is this his big chance? Hackforth-Jones is waiting for Tim's next serve. Will it be another ace? Jones has tried his best all through the match, but his best might not be good enough today. Just a minute! The umpire is making an announcement.

"Ladies and gentlemen, the game is abandoned due to poor light."

Can you believe that? We have had everything today: rain, snow, wind, a duck on court and now bad light! The crowd is very angry. People are throwing cushions, hats, programmes and ice creams at the umpire. The players have gone, so I think it's all over. Oh dear, here comes the rain; so it is now.

Compound words

● Look at the pictures and write down the **compound** words.

1.

cup   board   <u>cupboard</u>

2.  _____

3.  _____

4.  _____

5. _____

6.  _____

7.  _____

8.  _____

9.  _____

10.  _____

11. _____

12. _____

13. _____

14.  _____

15.  _____

16.  _____

● Use your dictionary to find some more compound words.

Poem parts

● Use your dictionary to find the meanings of these words:

verse _____

chorus _____

rhyming couplet _____

stanza _____

● Read the poem. Underline a verse in red, a chorus in blue, a stanza in yellow and a couplet in green.

The Jumblies

They went to sea in a Sieve, they did,
In a Sieve they went to sea:
In spite of all their friends could say,
On a winter's morn, on a stormy day,
In a Sieve they went to sea!
And when the Sieve turned round and round,
And every one cried, 'You'll all be drowned!'
They called aloud, 'Our Sieve ain't big,
But we don't care a button! we don't care a fig!
In a Sieve we'll go to sea!'
Far and few, far and few,
Are the lands where the Jumblies live;
Their heads are green, and their hands are blue,
And they went to sea in a Sieve.

They sailed away in a Sieve, they did,
In a Sieve they sailed so fast,
With only a beautiful pea-green veil
Tied with a riband by way of a sail,
To a small tobacco-pipe mast;
And every one said, who saw them go,
'O won't they be soon upset, you know!
For the sky is dark, and the voyage is long,
And happen what may, it's extremely wrong
In a Sieve to sail so fast!'
Far and few, far and few,
Are the lands where the Jumblies live;
Their heads are green, and their hands are blue,
And they went to sea in a Sieve.

Edward Lear

Points of view

Here are some arguments in favour of cycling as a form of transport. Choose the best points and put them into a letter to the local newspaper. Start 'Dear Editor...'

Cycling helps to keep you fit.

Cycling is often quicker than going by car in cities.

Bicycles are quieter than cars.

Cycling is cheaper than any other form of transport.

Bicycles don't need expensive motorways.

Bicycles take up less room than cars.

Cycling is a good way to see the countryside because it is slower than driving.

You don't have to pay tax to ride a bicycle.

Cycling does not cause pollution.

You can get to places by bicycle that a car cannot get to.

You don't need a large garage for a bicycle.

Purr-suasion

- How is this product being sold?
- What ways has the advertiser used to attract buyers?
- What is your opinion of this advertisement?
- Design an advertisement of yourr own suaing similar tactics.

Making a new ending

The woodcutter arrived in the nick of time and killed the wolf.
Little Red Riding Hood was saved.

Use the frames below to write a different ending.

The woodcutter arrived at the cottage

Then

But

Finally

Writing up notes

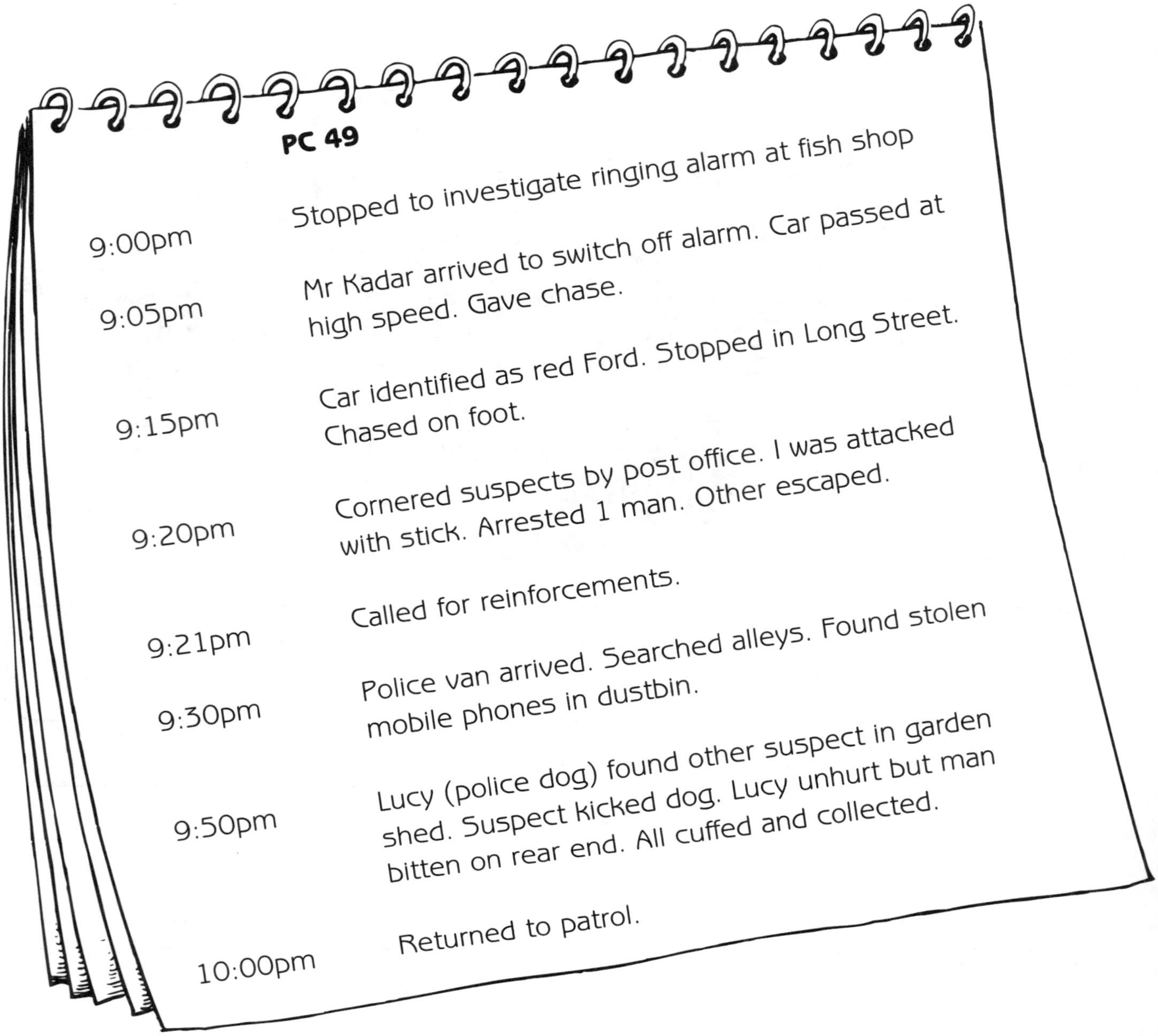

PC 49

9:00pm	Stopped to investigate ringing alarm at fish shop
9:05pm	Mr Kadar arrived to switch off alarm. Car passed at high speed. Gave chase.
9:15pm	Car identified as red Ford. Stopped in Long Street. Chased on foot.
9:20pm	Cornered suspects by post office. I was attacked with stick. Arrested 1 man. Other escaped.
9:21pm	Called for reinforcements.
9:30pm	Police van arrived. Searched alleys. Found stolen mobile phones in dustbin.
9:50pm	Lucy (police dog) found other suspect in garden shed. Suspect kicked dog. Lucy unhurt but man bitten on rear end. All cuffed and collected.
10:00pm	Returned to patrol.

Use the notes from the police notebook to write a full report of the crime.

_____

_____

_____

_____

_____

_____

_____

_____

Edit this

Use a red pen or pencil to edit this passage down so that it is more precise. Cross out repetitions and unnecessary information.

There was a knock at the door. Brian opened it because I was putting my lipstick on. I'd just bought a new colour, *Fungus Green*. Anyway, when he opened the door he found a group of excited people in the garden.

"Do you own a dog?" asked one of the women.

They were very excited.

"Yes," said Brian, "although we don't really own the dog we are just looking after it while our son Stephen is away on holiday. He has gone to Blackpool."

They were very excited.

"There's been an accident," a man said.

They were all so excited. We rushed outside. There was the poor dog whimpering in the road, but it seemed all right. I noticed she was wearing the collar I bought for her last Christmas. They were still very excited. Two women were running up and down the road crying.

"It has lost a leg!" one of the women cried. "Can you find it?"

Brian tried to calm her down. They were all very excited.

"It only had three legs to start with," he said.

After that we took the dog indoors and counted its legs, just to make sure, then it ate some jelly. It seemed OK.

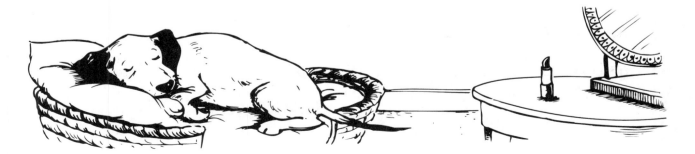

A simile poem

● Complete these **similes**. Look at the pictures for clues to the missing words.

He fled from the room…

…like a _____ in a rage,

…like a _____ in a battle,

…like a _____ in a stampede,

…like a _____ from a gun.

● Use your own ideas to complete this poem. You can add some more verses of your own.

The old man was…

…as wise as a _____,

…as proud as a _____,

…as hairy as a _____,

…as brave as a _____,

…as bold as a _____.

Groups of adjectives

● Put these **adjectives** into sets that have similar meanings.

happy	chilly	secure	content	wild
protected	mad	furious	freezing	unharmed
satisfied	bitter	livid	cool	frosty

pleased

angry

cold

safe

● Use a **thesaurus** to add to these groups.

warm

cautious

Placing adverbs

HOW?	WHERE?	WHEN?
merrily	nowhere	tomorrow
happily	there	earlier
swiftly	here	later
roughly	everywhere	yesterday
firmly		
carefully		

Write sentences that each contain at least one of the adverbs from the sets above.

What would you have done?

If you had been Goldilocks…

What would you have done on entering the house?

What would you have done next?

How do you think the story should end?

MATHS

By Year 4, the combination of repetition, reinforcement and progression results in the possibility of a mathematics Scheme of Work of gargantuan proportions. The supplement of maths examples given in the Numeracy Strategy runs to some 117 pages, roughly half of which show work for Year 4 children. Even if we had chosen one objective from each page to exemplify in this chapter, we would still have needed to produce about 50 photocopiables. Instead we have done what teachers will do when they are faced with so much curriculum ground to cover – we have made hard choices.

In the following sheets we have gone for range of cover rather than comprehensive or in-depth provision, both of which would be impossible within the scope of this book. A lot of basic number crunching, pencil and paper calculation and the like, is extensively and thoroughly covered in good primary maths textbooks, so we have made the not unreasonable assumption that you will have access to these. The sort of maths that you might do orally or 'on the blackboard' we have also chosen to ignore on the whole, for more obvious reasons. Nevertheless you will find useful and usable maths ideas here that will provide sound backup for your basic maths teaching and support a range of objectives identified in the Numeracy Strategy for Year 4 children.

If you require an overview of the mathematics programme for Year 4, then refer to the eleven bullet points in chapter two of the Numeracy Strategy (page 4). These identify the key objectives for the year. As the government has been a particularly prolific author on the subject of mathematics, you can get further information from the following (and subsequent publications): the *National Curriculum* and (1) *The Framework for Teaching Mathematics*; (2) *Mathematical Vocabulary*; (3) *Teaching Mental Calculation Strategies*; (4) *Standards in Mathematics*.

Words and numbers (page 40)

Objective: To know what each of the digits in a number represents and to partition numbers into Th H T and U.

What to do: The tasks on this sheet are straightforward, although you need to check that children understand the term 'digit' before they begin. The answers are: **1.** The biggest number is 65 431, the smallest 13 456; **2.** 54 320 and 20 345, unless you allow 2345 (ask the child who produces this to explain their answer); **3.** 6000, 700, 30, 1 and 7000.

Differentiation: Provide an abacus (a piece of equipment the children should have used previously) to support less able children who can construct each number on the abacus. Label Th, H, T and U if necessary.

Extension: Provide plenty of practice at writing down numbers that are given orally in both words and numerals.

Estimate (page 41)

Objective: To estimate a number up to around 250.

What to do: Clearly understanding the term *estimate* is vital here. Do not use the alternative *guess*, which can imply wild speculation (for example, *Guess who the next Prime Minister will be?*). All reasonable estimates should be accepted around 250; 300; 50; and 60. On the number line, estimates should be close to (in ascending order) 15, 45, and 75.

Differentiation: Less able children may need help in devising a strategy for estimation. Work with them in a group, help them to learn to divide up the space in their minds and count a section that will give a total that can then be multiplied appropriately to give an estimate. Ask them to think of other ways of estimating a quantity and give them simple practice at it. Estimate the number of children in the class, the number of scissors in the rack, pencils in the box, daffodils in the border and so on.

Extension: Give children plenty of practice at estimating numbers, volumes, weights and so on. In a class lesson, get children to explain their estimating strategies. Thinking out loud in this way is necessary for clarifying thought as well as modifying and improving mental strategies.

Approximate (page 42)

Objective: To make approximations and to round numbers to the nearest 10 or 100.

What to do: Skill in approximation needs a sound understanding of the number system. It is a necessary skill if children are to carry out complex pencil and paper calculations, or use calculators and arrive at sensible answers. This sheet is self-explanatory. Answers: 40kg, 440m, 40 miles, 30l (we round up when the number is halfway), 2360 miles, 30 minutes; 500, 500, 1600, 100, 900, 9400; 20 × 5, 700 + 200, and 50 × 20.

Differentiation: Some children may still need a visual prop. For most of the questions on this sheet working out the numbers on the class number line will be sufficient help.

Extension: Ask children to provide two answers to every arithmetic problem that they do (from maths books, perhaps) – the calculated answer and an answer rounded to the nearest 10, 100, or 1000 as instructed.

Negative integers (page 43)

Objective: To recognise and order negative and positive integers.

What to do: Firstly, the children need to be able to use the term *integer,* and know that negative numbers are integers too. The children also need to have been introduced to the notions of 'crossing the zero' and of number lines stretching in two directions. As the answers are to be written by the child on this sheet, any incorrect answers on the lines will be readily apparent.

Differentiation: Most children should manage this sheet but you may wish to prepare some children for the main activity by getting them to use parallel number lines to show an addition in the positive range, for example 'add 2'.

Extension: Give children a random selection of negative (or positive and negative) integers and ask them to put them in size order, for example 11, 31, –6, 5, –1, 17, 18, –3.

Equivalent fractions (1) (page 44)

Objectives: To use fraction notation; to begin to recognise the equivalence between fractions.

What to do: You may wish to do some examples with the whole class first. Get them to count the segments and to name the fractions. The answers are: $^2/_8$, $^2/_6$, $^4/_6$, $^2/_{10}$, $^6/_8$, $^1/_2$, $^4/_{10}$. Children may learn these equivalent fractions by rote.

Differentiation: An 'equivalent fraction board' is very useful apparatus for children who find it hard to visualise equivalent fractions or grasp the number relationships. These are available from educational equipment suppliers, or you can make them yourself out of stiff card or thin wood. Children can then handle the equivalent fractions and physically compare them to make the equivalence.

Extension: Children can make equivalent fraction charts showing families of fractions: halves, quarters, eighths; or thirds, sixths, twelfths, for example.

Equivalent fractions (2) (page 45)

Objectives: To use fraction notation; to begin to recognise the equivalence between fractions.

What to do: This is similar to, but more demanding than, the last sheet. The instructions are clear although children who struggle to understand the concept of equivalence may have difficulty carrying them out. The answers are : $^1/_4$, $^2/_4$, $^6/_8$, $^1/_3$. The rest must be marked visually.

Differentiation: This sheet does demand a level of understanding of equivalence beyond the basic $^1/_2 = ^2/_4$. Let the less confident children use equivalence boards and work with a partner to tackle this sheet.

Extension: Challenge children to order fractions by size. For most children this should be a practical challenge only. *Who will have most strawberry tart, a person who has ⅓ or a person who has ¼? Who has most orange juice, a child with a half-empty glass or a child with one that is half full? Mamie still has half her teeth, Natalie has a quarter of hers. Who has the most teeth?*

Decimal places (page 46)

Objective: To read and write decimal fractions.

What to do: Children who have been introduced to decimals should be able to attempt this sheet. Do not use it 'cold'. Introducing decimals is best done by using a model that children know, for example our currency system. The answers are: (the first question must be marked visually); £4.52; £2.22; £17.36; £5.25; £6.94; £9.62; 2.36 metres; 4.86 metres; 1.32 metres; 0.26 metres; 92.32 metres; 4.11 metres.

Differentiation: Additional teaching and support may need to be given to some groups of children who struggle to use the decimal number line. For the other questions, differentiate by giving apparatus (money, a metre stick) and additional adult attention.

Extension: More practice of the same is the best extension to this sheet. Let children deal with other decimal quantities, such as weight and volume.

Check it out! (page 47)

Objective: To check calculations using the inverse operation.

What to do: Make sure that children understand that addition reverses subtraction (and vice versa) and that division reverses multiplication (and vice versa). Explain the two examples at the top of the sheet and how they must use one of these methods to check the calculations below. The easiest way to check whether children are using the correct method is visually. This is the most important part of the sheet and arithmetical errors are not so significant. The sequence of correct and incorrect answers is as follows, starting with the first calculation: correct; correct; correct; incorrect; correct; incorrect; correct; incorrect; correct; incorrect; correct; and correct.

Differentiation: Where children experience difficulty they will need additional teaching support. Ask them to explain how they are tackling each calculation. Errors can usually be picked up quite easily and often children will self-correct.

Extension: Practice and yet more practice is needed if the processes are to become properly established in the children's minds. Ask children to double-check their answers when doing less demanding oral calculations in class. This should also be done out loud.

Number problems (page 48)

Objective: To use arithmetical operations appropriately to solve word problems involving numbers in real life.

What to do: Ironically, words that usually clarify seem to confuse when mixed with numbers. Make sure that children approach these 'problems' in a logical way. It often helps to write down the number elements of the problems separately, for example 8 (legs), 13 (spiders). Then: legs (altogether) = 8 × 13, becomes clearer. The answers are: 104 legs; the following Monday; 13 spoonfuls; 24 children; 17.

Differentiation: Provide any apparatus that might be useful for less able children, such as plastic cubes for spider's legs so that the mental problem can take on a physical form. Explaining out loud is very useful but is demanding of adult time. This is not a good co-operative exercise because inevitably co-operation allows some children not to engage their brains.

Extension: Give children a number statement, such as 24 − 7 = 17 and ask them to devise a story to explain the statement. For example, *There were 24 fairies in the wood. Seven got married to garden gnomes. How many were there left?*

Put it another way (page 49)

Objectives: To use vocabulary related to measures; to know relationships between familiar units.

What to do: 'Learn and remember' is the key to this sheet. Children might learn and remember the 'boxed' facts before attempting the sheet proper. This could be a homework task. The answers are: **1.** 5kg 322g; **2.** 2kg 129g; **3.** 9kg 3g; **4.** 10kg 42g; **5.** 2m 26cm; **6.** 5m 72cm; **7.** 14m 35cm; **8.** 9m 4cm; **9.** 2l 467ml; **10.** 1l 324ml; **11.** 5l 100ml; **12.** 6l 8ml.

Differentiation: Where sensible you should allow children to see the quantities involved – all the quantities on the sheet could probably be replicated (the grams will pose the biggest problem). Children will need to be able to read and understand numbers that run into thousands before attempting this.

Extension: Reverse the process. Give children their answers and ask them to convert the quantities back into the other form (without recourse to the original sheet).

Measuring scales (page 50)

Objective: To read a scale with a suitable degree of accuracy.

What to do: Most children should be able to read and follow the instructions here. They should write their answers on the lines on the sheet. Answers: **1.** 450ml; **2.** 1.5kg; **3.** 47 seconds; **4.** 120ml; **5.** 55cm.

Differentiation: Let less able children replicate each of the measures (you should possess identical or similar measuring equipment). They should measure the quantities for real but you may still need to support them by having adult help nearby.

Extension: Children could add their own problems to the sheet by colouring in a different quantity and then swapping sheets with a friend. You might also set up a range of measuring devices with set quantities on them so that children can read and record them. This could be an early morning activity or one to be carried out when a child is 'between tasks'.

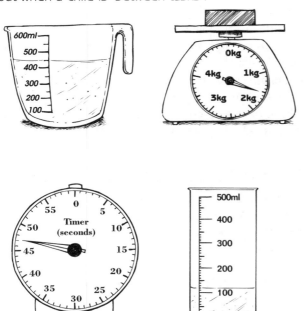

Journey round the edge: perimeter (page 51)

Objective: To measure and calculate the perimeter of simple shapes.

What to do: This activity presupposes the ability to use a ruler to draw a line and to measure accurately in centimetres. Children will need a centimetre ruler in good order as well as a pencil. Discuss the assignment with the class. Addition can be avoided if children measure on from the finishing point each time. Alternatively, children can write down the measurement of each side and add up the total at the end. However, children can easily get confused over perimeter so 'measuring on' will be the best option for most. The answers are: **1.** 15cm; **2.** 24cm; **3.** 20cm; **4.** 28cm; **5.** 12cm.

Differentiation: Provide close instruction on 'measuring on' to those children who find this exercise difficult. You could ask children to use a different-coloured pencil for each side and then to add up the measurements of each different-coloured length.

Extension: Set children 'estimate and measure' assignments, such as estimating the perimeter of the school hall, field, classroom, desktop and so on; then they measure and compare answers.

Tangram (page 52)

Objective: To understand that an area is unchanged no matter how the space is rearranged.

What to do: This is meant to be a fun exercise that emphasises the conservation of area. Let children play with the shapes to create people, buildings or whatever. In each case they should give their creation a name and state its area. The area of the tangram is 256cm². Ask the children how they propose to find the area of the shape. This should be done before cutting out and then by counting or calculation (depending on the ability of the children). The tangram is drawn on a centimetre-squared grid.

Differentiation: You may need to reiterate to less able children that the paper shape cannot and does not change in area however much its pieces are rearranged. If this is not understood then the idea needs to be revisited at a later date for them to grasp the concept of conservation of area.

Extension: Let children cut out tangrams from coloured paper (sticky paper is good but does not allow for the flipping over of pieces) and then display their best designs in a class gallery. In each case the area of the shape should be stated clearly.

Make a date (page 53)

Objective: To know and use the vocabulary related to dates and time.

What to do: The sheet is self-explanatory although you should have a current calendar for the children to refer to when necessary.

Differentiation: Less able children should work in pairs and should have ready access to a calendar.

Extension: Get children to make a list of all the words that they can find to do with the measurement of time over days, months and years. The obvious should be there, for example *month, week, year,* but there are many others, such as *season, autumn, night, noon, yesterday, millennium, am, pm, leap year, century* and so on. This could be a task for homework.

Time for TV (page 54)

Objective: To read and calculate time from timetables.

What to do: Show children a printed TV schedule (*TV Times* or similar). Challenge them to use it – could they find out when their favourite programme is on using the TV listings? Then let them work on the sheet, which is based on a real extract. The answers are: **1.** 1 hour; **2.** 1 hour 10 minutes; **3.** *Relatives* by 5 minutes; **4.** 3:22; **5.** 4 hours if you assume that the News and Weather is watched at 6:00 for ten minutes, but you should accept 3 hours 50 minutes, which excludes the latter. Ask the children to explain how they arrived at their answers.

Differentiation: This could usefully be tackled by a small group of children working together supportively.

Extension: Set children questions to answer about the current TV schedule: *How long will xxx last tonight? What is on at 7:00pm tomorrow?* And so on.

Put Polly in a polygon (page 55)

Objective: To name and classify polygons.

What to do: Children who have learned the terms used on this sheet should manage to follow the instructions without difficulty. Three shapes do not house Polly. Children must name the polygon as well as drawing Polly or the exercise is worthless.

Differentiation: Provide a reference sheet or chart that clearly defines and illustrates the terms used on the sheet. Less able children will need to refer to this.

Extension: Provide children with sets of coloured polygons (these are available commercially but can be made). Ask them to sort the shapes into sets according to any criteria you choose, such as triangles/ quadrilaterals or regular/irregular. Get them to draw round and name all the shapes as precisely as possible, for example not just *triangle* but *regular triangle*.

Building with cubes (page 56)

Objective: To visualise 3-D shapes from 2-D drawings.

What to do: This is an interesting exercise in visual perception and children should attempt to follow the instructions without using apparatus in the first instance. The answers are: 16; 7; 8; 12; and 14.

Differentiation: For less able children this can be turned into a concrete exercise. Give them building blocks and let them replicate the shapes, then count the blocks used.

Extension: Get children to work in pairs. Each child takes it in turn to create a building using cubes placed squarely face-to-face. The other child has to estimate how many cubes have been used and then check their answer by counting.

Ordered pairs (page 57)

Objective: To use coordinates.

What to do: If necessary, play a version of noughts and crosses (tic-tac-toe) with the class, using a numbered grid. Remember to use the numbered lines not the squares. Then children should be able to cope with the task on the sheet. The answers are best written alongside the letters on the grid. The answers are: **A** (1,2); **B** (1,7); **C** (2,6); **D** (3,3); **E** (4,8); **F** (4,5); **G** (5,4); **H** (6,7); **I** (7,1); **J** (8,9); **K** (8,6); **L** (8,1).

Differentiation: Tic-tac-toe, Battleships and other location games may need to be played often and regularly to establish the rule with some children. Reiterate the rule 'in at the door before going up the stairs'. Insist that less able children learn this by rote.

Extension: Draw simple shapes on centimetre-squared paper and ask children to give the coordinates of specific points, such as the corners of a square, the eye of a cat, the jewel in a crown and so on.

Horizontal and vertical (page 58)

Objective: To recognise and identify simple examples of horizontal and vertical.

What to do: This is confirmation of understanding of the terms *vertical* and *horizontal*. The sheet should be marked by reference to the pictures.

Differentiation: Let less able children work in pairs on this activity. A prominent display illustrating the two terms is worth having as children can check their answers with reference to the display, for example checking the parachutist against the displayed vertical line.

Extension: Ask the children to draw three pictures (of each direction) to illustrate vertical and horizontal. A good homework task.

Sizing up angles (page 59)

Objective: To place a set of angles in order of size.

What to do: Ordering is what is required, not precise measurement in degrees. All the angles are less than 180°. Children record their answers by putting the letters in the order of their choice. The answers are: **1.** A, D, C, B; **2.** B, D, C, A; **3.** A, B, D, C; **4.** D, C, B, A.

Differentiation: For those who find this difficult you could enlarge the sheet (it does not alter the angles) then cut out each question in turn. The angles can be cut out and physically compared for size.

Extension: Children should know and remember that a whole turn is 360°; a quarter turn is 90° (which is a right-angle); half a right-angle is 45°; that the angles in the corners of squares and rectangles are 90° and that the angles in an equilateral triangle are 60°. This would make a useful homework task.

A question of degrees (page 60)

Objective: To make and describe turns using compass directions.

What to do: Although the sheet is uncomplicated,

children will find it difficult if they are given it cold. You will need to remind them of turns and angles (see previous activity, 'Sizing up angles') and physically move pointers, hands on a clock, children(!) to demonstrate angles as rotation. The answers are: 90 degrees, clockwise; 45 degrees, anti-clockwise; 90 degrees, anti-clockwise; 45 degrees, clockwise. For the second question: 90 degrees, 180 degrees, 270 degrees, 360 degrees, 135 degrees and 335 degrees.

Differentiation: Form a supervised group and carry out the turns for real with those children who need more help.

Extension: You can set up similar exercises using the hands of a clock. Ask the children: *How many degrees does the large hand move through from 1:00 to 1:30?* And so on.

Sort by sets (page 61)

Objective: To use a Venn diagram to sort and display information about numbers or shapes.

What to do: Children will be familiar with the use of sets from an early age. This is simply sorting by numerical attribute. These Venn diagrams do involve placing some numbers in both sets simultaneously and you may need to remind children of what happens in these cases by reference to the numbers already placed in the sets. The exercise is best marked by visual reference.

Differentiation: Unless the child's knowledge of the number system is very slight, the selection of numbers should pose no problems. It is as well to supervise less able children fairly closely at the start to make sure that they understand how the Venn diagrams work.

Extension: Similar problems can be devised along the same lines for more practice.

Get sorted! (page 62)

Objective: To sort and display information about numbers and shapes using a Carroll diagram.

What to do: The Carroll diagram is slightly more complicated than the Venn diagram and children may be unfamiliar with it. Demonstrate how it works by sorting quantities in the way shown on the sheet. NB: The first criterion is always the negation of the second and vice versa. The easiest way to mark this sheet is by visual reference.

Differentiation: Differentiation will be by the amount of supervision given, for although the numerical task is quite simple, children may well find difficulty sorting out the diagram. Be on hand to support them.

Extension: Produce blank two-way Venn diagrams and provide children with further examples to sort along the lines shown.

Words and numbers

● Make the biggest number you can using all these digits.

6   1   5   4   3   _____

Make the smallest number using the same digits. _____

Write the smallest number in words.

_____

● Do the same using these digits.

2   0   4   5   3

Biggest number   _____

Smallest number   _____

Smallest number in words _____

● Put the correct numbers in the boxes.

6531 = [   ] + 500 + 30 + 1

1786 = 1000 + [   ] + 80 + 6

4932 = 4000 + 900 + [   ] + 2

5811 = 5000 + 800 + 10 + [   ]

7634 = [   ] + 600 + 30 = 4

Estimate

● How many dots? _____

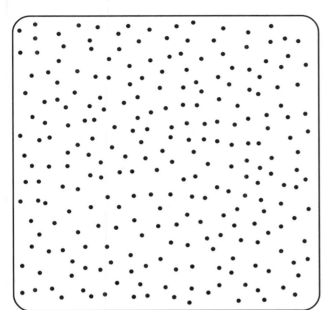

● How many letters? _____

There was a table set out under a tree in front of the house, and the March Hare and the Hatter were having tea at it: a Dormouse was sitting between them, fast asleep, and the other two were using it as a cushion, resting their elbows on it, and talking over its head. "Very uncomfortable for the Dormouse," thought Alice: "only as it's asleep, I suppose it doesn't mind."

● How many arrows? _____

● How many bricks? _____

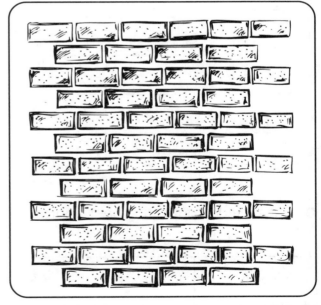

● Estimate which numbers the arrows are pointing at here.

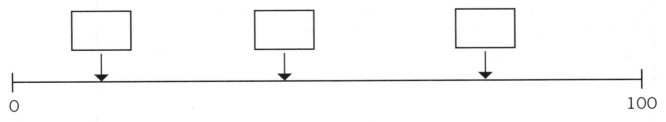

0   100

Approximate

● Round these measurements to the nearest 10.

36kg   _____

437m   _____

42 miles   _____

25l   _____

2364 miles   _____

31 minutes   _____

● Round these numbers to the nearest 100.

537   _____

493   _____

1631   _____

97   _____

876   _____

9430   _____

● Put a circle round the best approximation for:

18 × 5	80 × 6	8 × 60	88 × 5	20 × 5
703 + 196	700 + 200	700 + 100	800 + 200	
49 × 19	40 × 10	50 × 10	40 × 20	50 × 20

Negative integers

A **whole number** is called an **integer**.

● Number lines can go in two directions. Fill in the missing integers on this line.

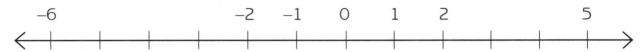

−6   −2   −1   0   1   2   5

● What is the temperature on this thermometer?

● Use a coloured pencil and a ruler to complete this diagram showing **subtract 3**. Start on the left number line. Keep going until you run out of number line!

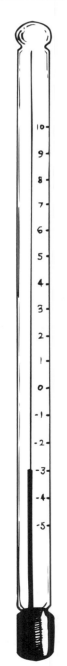

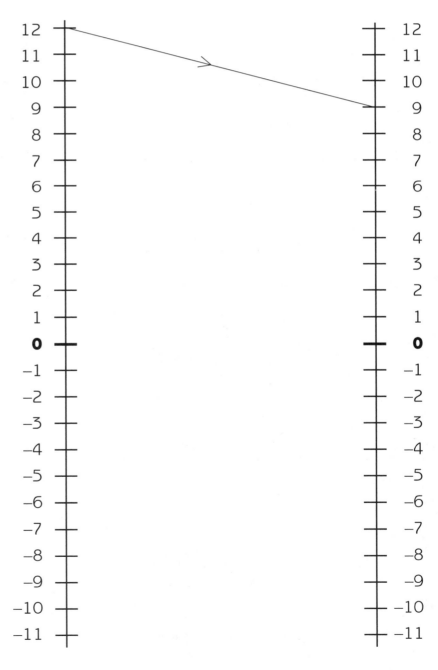

Equivalent fractions (1)

● Colour in the equivalent fraction and write its name. The first one is done for you.

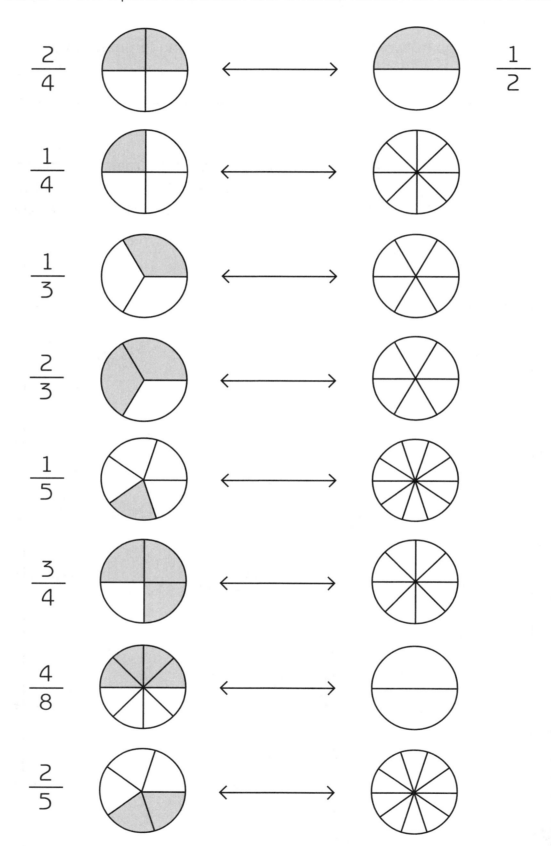

● Learn these equivalent fractions. Test your memory with a friend.

Equivalent fractions (2)

● Work out these equivalent fractions.

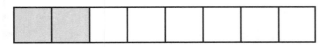 $\dfrac{2}{8}$ shaded → $\dfrac{}{4}$

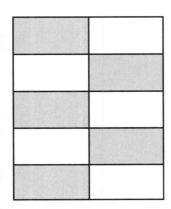 $\dfrac{5}{10}$ shaded → $\dfrac{}{4}$

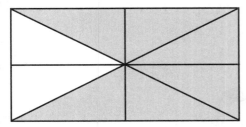 $\dfrac{3}{4}$ shaded → $\dfrac{}{8}$

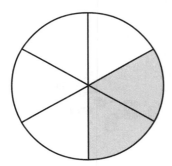 $\dfrac{2}{6}$ shaded → $\dfrac{}{3}$

● Shade the following fractions.

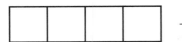 $\dfrac{1}{2}$

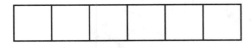 $\dfrac{2}{3}$

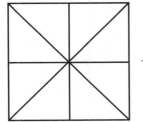 $\dfrac{6}{8}$

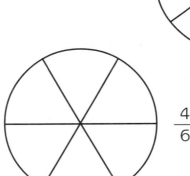 $\dfrac{1}{5}$

$\dfrac{4}{6}$

Decimal places

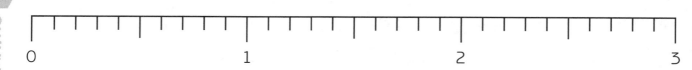

0   1   2   3

● Put these decimals in the right places on the number line above.

2.5
2.8
0.7
1.6
0.4
1.3

● Write these amounts of money in pounds like this: 365p = £3.65

452p = _____

222p = _____

1736p = _____

525p = _____

694p = _____

962p = _____

● Write these centimetres in metres like this: 359cm = 3.59m

236cm = _____

486cm = _____

132cm = _____

26cm = _____

9232cm = _____

411cm = _____

Check it out!

We can check calculations by the following methods:

A 321 – 45 = 276   CHECK   276 + 45 = ⬚321 ✓

B 30 × 5 = 150   CHECK   150 ÷ 5 = ⬚30 ✓

● Use method **A** or **B** to check these calculations.
   (Watch out! They are not all correct!)

465 – 82 = 383   CHECK →   _____

91 – 28 = 63   CHECK →   _____

25 × 6 = 150   CHECK →   _____

12 × 8 = 88   CHECK →   _____

40 × 4 = 160   CHECK →   _____

633 – 66 = 566   CHECK →   _____

● How would you check the following?

158 + 37 = 195   CHECK →   _____

524 + 125 = 651   CHECK →   _____

120 ÷ 4 = 30   CHECK →   _____

32 ÷ 2 = 16   CHECK →   _____

Number problems

● A spider has 8 legs.
Daniel keeps 13 spiders as pets.
How many legs altogether?

_____

● Ruth loves chocolate biscuits.
There are 36 in the barrel. She eats 5 on
Monday and the same number every day
until there are none left. On what day does
she finish the last one?

_____

● 5 people live in Eve's house.
They all take 3 spoonfuls of sugar in their
tea, except Eve who takes only one.
How many spoonfuls for the whole family
when they all drink tea?

_____

● Half of Delilah's class were born in
Israel, a quarter were born in Ireland,
the rest were born in Hendon.
There are 32 in the class.
How many were not born in Hendon?

_____

● Jezebel adds 16 to a
number and gets 33.
What number did she
start with?

_____

Put it another way

Learn and remember:

1 metre = 100 centimetres   1 kilometre = 1000 metres

1 kilogram = 1000 grams   1 litre = 1000 millilitres

Write these measurements another way.

1. 5322 grams = ____5____ kilograms ___322___ grams

2. 2129 grams = _____ kilograms _____ grams

3. 9003 grams = _____ kilograms _____ grams

4. 10042 grams = _____ kilograms _____ grams

5. 2.26 metres = _____ metres _____ centimetres

6. 5.72 metres = _____ metres _____ centimetres

7. 14.35 metres = _____ metres _____ centimetres

8. 9.04 metres = _____ metres _____ centimetres

9. 2467 millilitres = _____ litres _____ millilitres

10. 1324 millilitres = _____ litres _____ millilitres

11. 5100 millilitres = _____ litres _____ millilitres

12. 6008 millilitres = _____ litres _____ millilitres

Learn and remember:

1 mile is longer than 1 kilometre but less than 2 kilometres.

Measuring scales

Read these measures as accurately as you can.

1.

2.

3.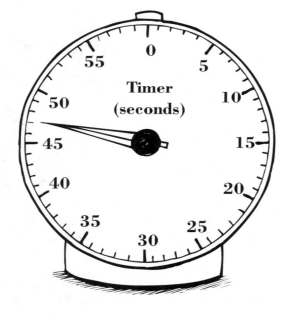

4.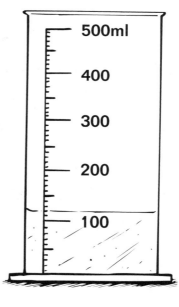

5.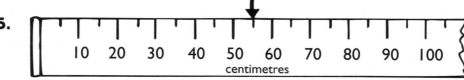

centimetres

Journey round the edge: perimeter

● Draw round each of these shapes with a coloured pencil.
● Measure how far your pencil travelled in each case.

1.

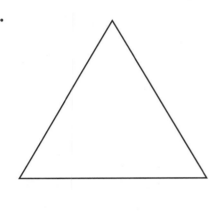

2.

3.

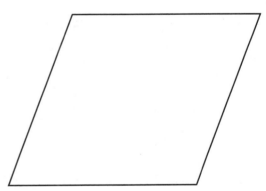

4.

5.

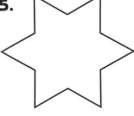

Tangram

● What is the area of this square? _____

● This is a Chinese puzzle called a **tangram**. Colour the pieces and cut them out. Rearrange them to make interesting shapes. What area does your new shape have?

_____

● Can you put the square back together again?

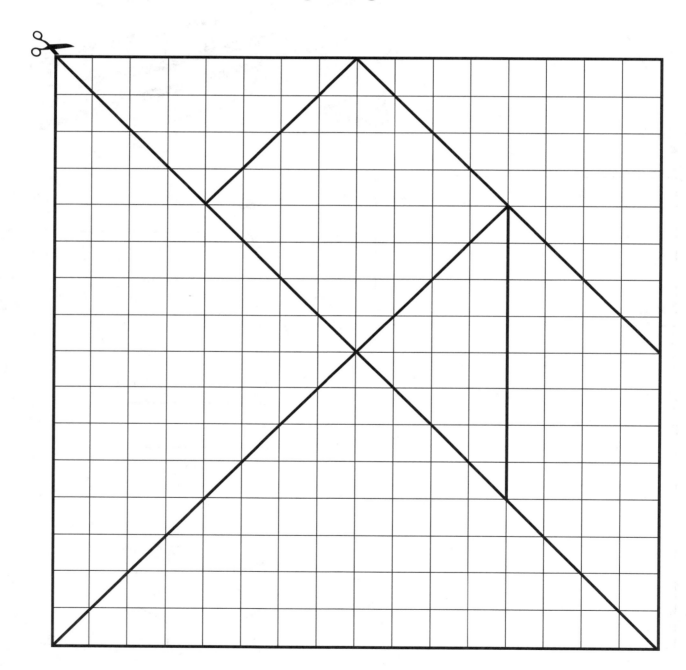

Make a date

Recite and learn this rhyme about the number of days in each month of the year.

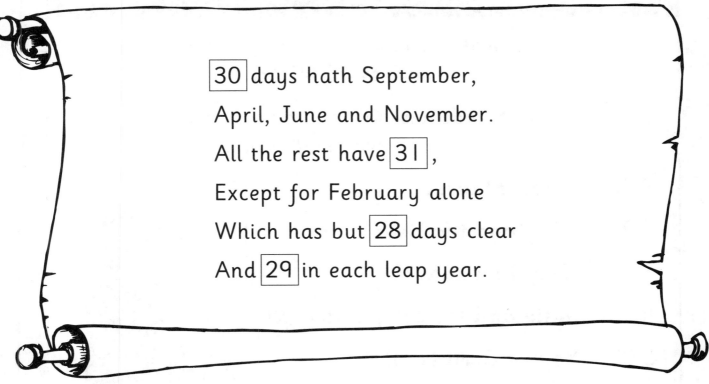

30 days hath September,

April, June and November.

All the rest have 31,

Except for February alone

Which has but 28 days clear

And 29 in each leap year.

1. How many days in June? _____

2. How many days in March? _____

3. How many days in December? _____

4. How many days in February in a leap year? _____

5. How many days in February this year? _____

6. Write down the day, month and year of your birthday.

_____

7. If September 1st is a Monday, what day is September 7th? _____

and what day is the last day in September? _____

8. December 15th is a Monday. What day is Christmas Day? _____

Time for TV

TV MONDAY 12TH MARCH

2:10   **Heartthrob**   *Drama. A robbery brings love to PC 49. (R)*

3:10   **News Headlines** *Followed by regional news and weather.*

3:20   **Small Planets**

3:30   **Eddy and the Bear**

3:45   **Ugly Martians** *(R)*

4:40   **Sally and the Silly Witch** *(R)*

5:05   **You've Been Had!** *(R)*

5:30   **Relatives** *Brad and Sheila have an argument.*

6:00   **News and Weather.**

1. How long does *Heartthrob* last? _____

2. How long from the end of *Small Planets* to the start of *Sally and the Silly Witch*?

_____

3. Which is the longer programme, *You've Been Had!* or *Relatives*?

_____

4. If *Heartthrob* lasted 12 minutes longer than planned, what time would it finish?

_____

5. If you watched all of these programmes, for how long would you have

watched TV? _____

Put Polly in a polygon

Here is Polly in a polygon. A **polygon** is a flat shape with at least 3 straight sides.
This polygon is a **quadrilateral**.

● Draw Polly inside
these polygons and
write the name of each
polygon underneath:

(a square)   (a heptagon)   (an equilateral triangle)

(a rectangle)   (a hexagon)   (a pentagon)

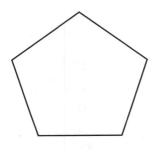

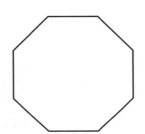

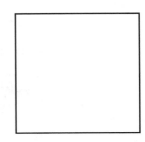

_____   _____   _____

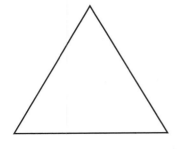

_____   _____   _____

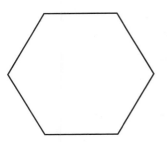

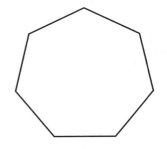

_____   _____   _____

Building with cubes

● Look at these drawings. What is the least number of cubes needed to build these models?

1. Number of cubes _____

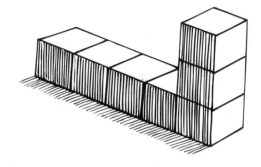

2. Number of cubes _____

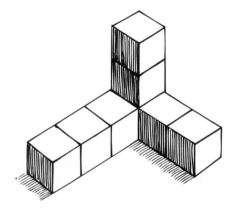

3. Number of cubes _____

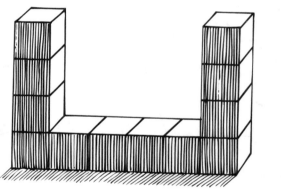

4. Number of cubes _____

● Estimate how many cubes you would need to build this model. _____

● Build it and check your estimate.

● What is the difference?

_____

Ordered pairs

● Two numbers are used to describe a point on a grid. Look carefully and notice which number comes first.

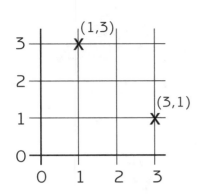

Remember we go in the door

before going up the stairs.

● Use pairs of numbers (in the correct order) to describe the points labelled A to L. Write your answers by the points on the grid.

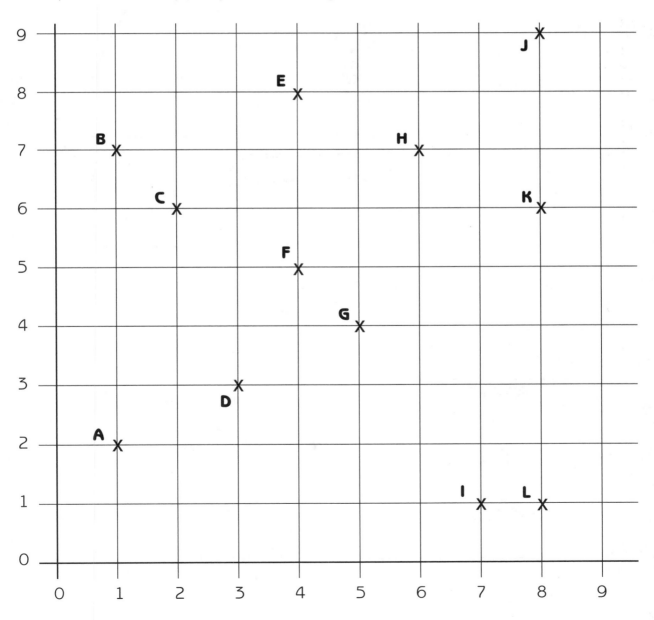

Horizontal and vertical

Which is which? Write the correct word by each picture.
Is the object **horizontal** or **vertical**?

The plane is _____

The parachutist is

_____

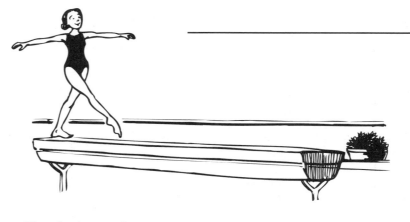

The balance beam is _____

The flagpole is

The girl is _____

_____

The table top is _____

The water is

The table leg is _____

_____

Sizing up angles

Put these sets of angles in size order, starting with the smallest.

1.

 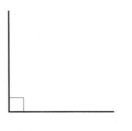 

A   B   C   D

Size order _____

2.

A   B   C   D

Size order _____

3.

   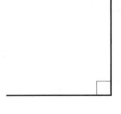

A   B   C   D

Size order _____

4.

A   B   C   D

Size order _____

A question of degrees

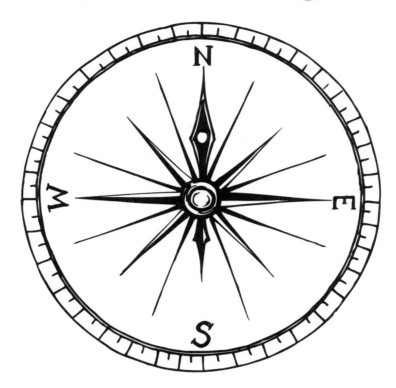

● If you were facing **due east**, how many degrees would you turn through to face (by the shortest route):

south   _____   direction of turn   _____

north east   _____   direction of turn   _____

north   _____   direction of turn   _____

south east   _____   direction of turn   _____

● Face **north**. Turn **clockwise** to face the following directions. How many degrees do you turn through?

east   _____

south   _____

west   _____

north (again)   _____

south east   _____

north west   _____

Sort by sets

● Add these to the diagram:
51, 54, 33, 27, 41, 58, 50, 53

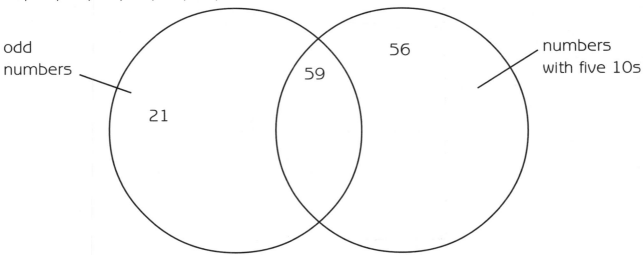

odd
numbers

21

59

56

numbers
with five 10s

● Add these to the diagram:
8, 20, 15, 25, 45, 60, 35

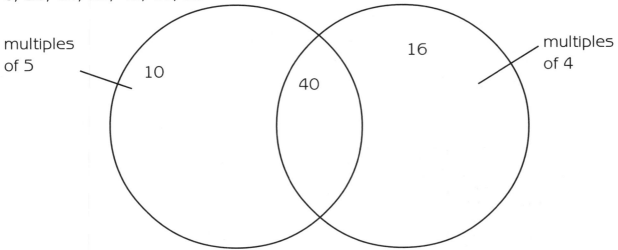

multiples
of 5

10

40

16

multiples
of 4

● Add these to the diagram:
30, 25, 9, 27, 45, 18, 40

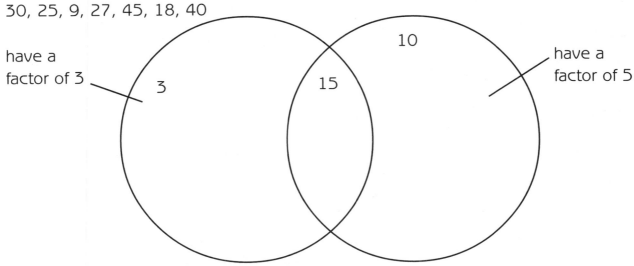

have a
factor of 3

3

15

10

have a
factor of 5

Get sorted!

● Add these to the diagram: 6, 27, 9, 17, 1, 25, 2, 12, 16, 20, 23

	multiples of 2	not multiples of 2
multiples of 3	24 30	3 21
not multiples of 3	4 26	19 5

● Add these to the diagram: 40, 47, 21, 44, 26, 45, 48, 27, 31, 36

	odd	even
numbers that have four 10s	41	46
numbers that do not have four 10s	33	28

● Add these to the diagram:

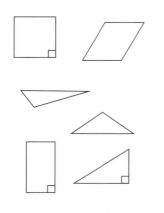

	has a right angle	does not have a right angle
has four sides	▭	▱
does not have four sides	◣	△

SCIENCE

Year 4 science is both fascinating and challenging. If we take the QCA Scheme of Work as our guide, then children may encounter phrases such as *thermal conductor* and *thermal insulator*, or have to identify the main features of vertebrates and distinguish between habitats. The QCA scheme is allocated 66 hours, which is a great deal of curriculum time. Teachers will need to be well prepared in terms of knowledge and equipment to make sure that this time is not wasted, for example have you got a variety of thermometers in your school, including a temperature sensor for your computer?

Although we cannot help with equipment, we can help with ideas and activities, so many of these sheets direct the child to 'do' rather than to work solely with pencil and paper. We strongly recommend that you ensure you are properly prepared before you hand out the sheets. We have made the assumption that our assignments will be set firmly in the context of observation and experiment. The sheets broadly cover the content suggested in the QCA Scheme of Work and within it, those objectives that worksheets are best able to support.

The National Curriculum science 'contexts' are Sc2 'Life processes and living things'; Sc3 'Materials and their properties'; and Sc4 'Physical processes'. Sc1 'Scientific enquiry', sets out the skills and principles to be taught through these 'contexts'. For Year 4, the QCA propose six units which are: 4A Moving and growing; 4B Habitats; 4C Keeping warm; 4D Solids, liquids and how they can be separated; 4E Friction; 4F Circuits and conductors. The worksheets in this book follow progressively from the worksheets in previous volumes, one advantage of which is that differentiated work can be created very easily using material prepared for other year groups.

The human skeleton (page 68)

Objectives: To understand that humans have bony skeletons inside their bodies that grow as they grow; to locate major bones in the human body.

What to do: What children should notice above all else is *growth* and this should be confirmed by the activity that they undertake. Full calcification of a human skeleton takes about 20 years, at which point it contains about 5kg of mineral salts. A large chart of a skeleton, a drawing of one, or even a model skeleton, is essential teaching equipment for this study. The answers to naming the parts can be checked by reference to a chart or model. The ribs (12 pairs) should be self-evident, as should the skull (containing 29 bones including 14 in the face and the stirrup bones

in the ear – which are the smallest in the body). The femur is the thigh bone (the largest in the body); the pelvis supports most of the body weight when standing and the breast bone (sternum) is, of course, in the breast.

Differentiation: Ideal support for children struggling to learn the names of the main parts of the skeleton is a model skeleton that can be assembled and disassembled. This equipment is available commercially and enables children to play with the bones, become familiar with their construction and learn their names.

Extension: Get children to compare human skeletons with those of other vertebrates. Children are usually quite familiar with dinosaur skeletons so let them compare these. Visit a museum that has suitable displays of skeletons. Check locally, although the best collections (of dinosaurs) are in London (Natural History Museum) and Oxford. The next sheet also provides useful extension to this assignment.

Vertebrates (page 69)

Objectives: To examine and to raise questions about different bony skeletons; to make observations and comparisons of particular features.

What to do: Children should examine the drawings carefully. The text draws their attention to the connection between skeletal structure and the nature of the animal. The answers to the identification task are: a hare and a cat. Draw children's attention to the

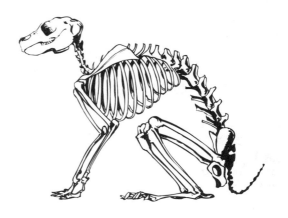

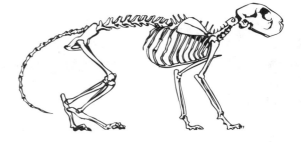

fact that the names of bones are common to a range of creatures even where the bones vary in shape or length. Can they spot the femur on the hare? You may wish to provide the children with copies of photocopiable page 68 to help them complete the last question on the sheet.

Differentiation: Let this activity be as 'hands on' as possible. Use models, displays of real bones, visits to museums and so on to make the project come alive. You might provide less able children with several pictures of animals (not their skeletons) including a cat and hare, and ask them to match the animals to the skeleton.

Extension: Challenge the children to locate and name (using information from the previous activity, 'The human skeleton', or reference books) as many bones as they can on the skeletons shown.

Animals without bony skeletons (page 70)

Objective: To understand that all bodies need support but that not all animals have internal skeletons to do this.

What to do: Point out that all creatures have bodies that need support in some way. What would happen if they did not have that support? Teach them the word *invertebrate*. Answers to the exercises are: snail – support on the outside of the body, worm – by its skin and the soil in which it lives, crab – skeleton on the outside, locust – external shell.

Differentiation: Lots of back-up reference material needs to be provided for less able children, although it should be available for all so that children can extend their knowledge.

Extension: Ask children to investigate invertebrates. Let them draw, name and explain how each body is supported. A possible homework task.

Muscles and movement (page 71)

Objective: To learn that animals with skeletons have muscles attached to their bones and that a muscle has to contract (shorten) to make a bone move.

What to do: Talk about the information on this sheet. It is important that children understand that movement is only generated when a muscle *shortens*; they cannot push, which is why muscles work in pairs. The apparatus demonstrates this. You need to have this built, tried and tested before undertaking this task. NB For safety reasons, the springs must not be too powerful. Children should experiment with the equipment and record their observations.

Differentiation: Small group or paired work is the best way to tackle this sheet and some children would benefit from adult support. Observations might be recorded on tape, given orally to the class or written down by an adult if this proves to be a stumbling block to the science.

Extension: Ask children to record their observations when muscles work hard (exercise) and when a person is at rest. Collect words relating to both, for example *relax, tired, hot, contract.*

Organisms (page 72)

Objectives: To learn the term *organism*; to sort organisms into plants and animals.

What to do: Introduce the term *organism* to cover both plants and animals – a general term for all living things (fungi are now placed in a separate category from plants and animals). The exercise is easily marked by visual reference.

Differentiation: Let less confident children work in pairs on this activity. Children may find this a difficult exercise and you should discuss the answers in a plenary session. They may also enjoy cutting out the pictures and sticking them into a book or folder according to the correct category.

Extension: Challenge children to extend the lists further. A possible task for homework.

Habitats (page 73)

Objectives: To identify types of habitats; to recognise that different animals are found in different habitats.

What to do: Explain the instructions on the sheet. Answers are open-ended. You might wish to dismiss foolish answers first (a cow up a tree – it fell there after trying to jump over the Moon). Stress that you are looking for habitats that suit particular organisms.

Differentiation: Focus on making sure that less able children understand the term *habitat.*

Extension: Get children to draw up a list of different types of habitat, such as *under a stone, a lawn.* Give them a list of organisms to locate. *Where would you* find a woodlouse? A *tadpole*? Fieldwork is called for here and you should find time to look at different habitats for real. Most schools set up a range of habitats deliberately for just this purpose; if yours does not have a pond or 'wild area' then investigate access to alternative sites nearby.

Identification keys (page 74)

Objectives: To group organisms according to observed features; to use keys to identify particular plants and animals.

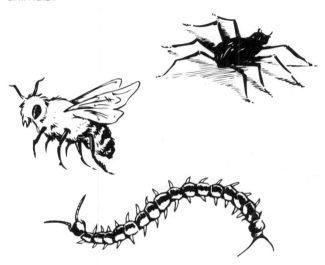

What to do: This is a fairly simple task but is made complex by explanation, especially on paper. You should talk through the task with the class first to make sure they understand what is expected of them. They will need further sheets of paper to devise their own 'key'. The answers to the first task are self-evident: **1.** bee; **2.** centipede; **3.** spider. (A harvestman is commonly known as a daddy-long-legs; a false scorpion has no sting.)

Differentiation: More pictures and reference books should be provided as support, although some children may need further adult support in framing the questions in a *yes/no* form.

Extension: Select further creatures or plants for which children can devise identification keys.

Food chains (page 75)

Objective: To understand what a food chain is and that most food chains start with a green plant.

What to do: Make sure that the terms are understood – *food chain, producer*. The answers to the set task are: leaves – worms – birds – cats. The producer: leaves.

Differentiation: Underpin children's understanding of food chains by showing lots of examples. There are videos and CD-ROMs available. Provide books and reference material as support.

Extension: Choose a starting point in a particular habitat and get children to examine what food chains might arise there. For homework, ask children to define the words *prey* and *predator* and to describe examples of each.

Thermometers (page 76)

Objective: To understand that a thermometer measures how hot or cold things are (temperature).

What to do: This sheet requires observation and some book research. The thermometers are: a clinical thermometer, a forehead thermometer, a maximum and minimum thermometer (one that records the maximum and minimum temperatures over a set period) and a soil/dipping thermometer (thermostik). You should have examples of each to show the class.

Differentiation: Provide reference books (and help with using them) as support for those children that need it.

Extension: Carry out an experiment with a range of temperatures suitable for children to judge by touch, for example lukewarm water, cold water, an ice cube. Establish that touch is a way of judging temperature but that it is neither very accurate nor always safe. (Ice cubes should not be handled immediately after removal from a freezer.)

Wrap up! (page 77)

Objective: To get children to suggest ways to test how cold things can be kept cold.

What to do: For the first part of the activity, children need to explain how they would set up a fair test. They can write this down in the space provided on the sheet or explain it orally. Before the test is carried out you must be satisfied that it is safely and sensibly set up. You will also need to make sure that you have the materials and equipment required.

Differentiation: Less able children should work in closely supervised small groups or pairs.

Extension: Ask children to record the results of their tests using a block chart or other suitable tabulation. You may employ suitable computer software for this task.

Keeping solids and liquids apart (page 78)

Objective: To correctly classify materials as liquid or solid.

What to do: When the children have completed the task, discuss the answers. Note that it is the content of the containers that the children are being asked to identify. They will not find defining some of the examples easy. Hair spray? Ice cream? Salt? Note that a sponge is a solid that can change shape because of the air within it. Emphasise the tests suggested. At this stage children will not be aware that solid, liquid and gas are all states of matter into which every substance in the world can exist, given the right conditions. Even rock becomes liquid in a volcano. The answers from left to right are: L, S, L, S, L, L, S, S, S, S, L, S, L, L, S. The ambiguities should stimulate discussion.

Differentiation: Undoubtedly this task is best approached through discussion in small groups. Provide adult support to those groups that struggle to agree.

Extension: Ask the children to name some solids that behave like liquids in some ways. (For example, sand, salt and rice are solids but can be poured.)

Freezing, solidifying or melting

(page 79)

Objectives: To understand that the same material can exist as both a solid and a liquid; to know that melting, solidifying or freezing are changes that can be reversed and are the reverse of each other.

What to do: Children add the words *freezing* and *melting* to the appropriate arrows. The question by the chocolate should stimulate discussion about reversibility. This is best marked by visual reference. The answers to the cloze procedure sentences are: freezing, solidifying and melting.

Differentiation: 'F' and 'M' can be used instead of the full words if it helps to focus children's attention on the science rather than the writing task. The science is best reinforced by demonstration.

Extension: Each of these examples can be demonstrated in school. Ask children to think of other examples of freezing and melting.

Separate (1) (page 80)

Objective: To understand that solids can be mixed and that it is often possible to get the original materials back.

What to do: This is an experiment sheet. Make sure that you have the equipment and materials for children to carry out the tasks. The answers are open-ended, depending on the mix and method.

Differentiation: Some groups of children will need close supervision and occasional assistance from an adult.

Extension: You could extend the range of solids to be mixed and get children to tabulate their results in a suitable way. Can they think of any examples of the need to separate solids in everyday life? (Removing seeds from tomatoes in cooking, pips from lemons, tea leaves from a drink and so on.)

What happens when? (page 81)

Objective: To understand that changes occur when some solids are added to water.

What to do: Explain the instructions and the diagrams on the sheet. It is intended that children actually make the mixes described so you will need suitable containers as well as the materials listed.

Differentiation: Close supervision and support should be provided for the less competent.

Extension: Challenge children to describe the difference between melting and dissolving and to give examples of each.

Separate (2) (page 82)

Objective: To understand that when solids do not dissolve or react with water they can be separated by filtering.

What to do: Once again this is a sheet containing an experiment for which you will need to provide the equipment and materials. You may also need to explain the term *filtering* beforehand.

Differentiation: Some children will require close support and supervision coupled with help with the recording of their observations.

Extension: Ask children to give an example from home of each of the following: melting, dissolving, sieving and filtering.

Friction (page 83)

Objectives: To understand that the force between two moving surfaces is called friction; to group surfaces into *high friction* and *low friction*.

What to do: The sheet is self-explanatory. Answers are open-ended. The pictures on the sheet illustrate the difference – where there is maximum slide/lowest stick, such as with the ice-skating, the friction is lower. The opposite is high friction.

Differentiation: Make this a group assignment for those who require support.

Extension: Children might carry out any of a number of tests involving friction (you may wish to refer to reference and teaching books for further ideas). For example, children could devise tests to see which shape moves most easily through water.

Friction and forcemeters (page 84)

Objectives: To use a forcemeter carefully to measure forces; to learn that a *newton* is a unit of force; to understand that there is a force between an object and a surface that may prevent it from moving.

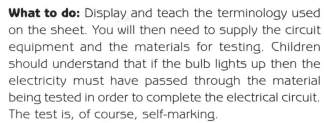

What to do: Provide children with suitable forcemeters and the facilities to carry out the tests described. You can explain to children that nothing in the universe will move unless it is acted on by a force, that is, something forces it to move.

Differentiation: Less able children will need to do this experiment with adult help in order to record and measure accurately.

Extension: Ask questions such as: *When you apply force to an object and make it move, why does it not go on moving forever?* (Because there are other forces such as friction, that slow it down.) Challenge children to find out what slows a ball down when it is thrown (friction of the air molecules).

Good conductors (page 85)

Objective: To construct a circuit to test which materials let electricity pass through.

What to do: Display and teach the terminology used on the sheet. You will then need to supply the circuit equipment and the materials for testing. Children should understand that if the bulb lights up then the electricity must have passed through the material being tested in order to complete the electrical circuit. The test is, of course, self-marking.

Differentiation: Supervise less able children to see that they do not get the 'wrong' results through inadequate management of the circuit – there must be no breaks other than those made deliberately.

Extension: Children should be allowed to test other materials and objects. Can they draw any conclusions? Those materials that conduct electricity are usually metal. Graphite in a pencil is a form of carbon, but not a metal, and is a good conductor of electricity.

Making and breaking (page 86)

Objectives: To understand that a complete circuit is needed for a device to work; to understand that a switch can be used to make or break a circuit.

What to do: Children can arrive at the solution to this problem by close examination of the maze – touching corners 1 and 2 will complete the circuit, touching the other two will not as they are not connected and the circuit will remain broken. Making a circuit like this is a valuable exercise – fun but also fiddly. Good equipment is essential. The maze can be made using strips of foil glued onto stiff cardboard. Make sure that your glue works! The circuit maze need not be as complicated as the one shown on the sheet. The last question on the sheet encourages the children to think about why we need switches. (The oven would overheat and so would the electricity bill!)

Differentiation: Encourage children to trace the connections on the maze using a coloured pencil if they do not find the answer readily apparent. Supervise the experiment closely.

Extension: Challenge children to make a simple switch that will turn the light on and off.

The human skeleton

Humans and other animals have bony skeletons inside their bodies. These animals are known as **vertebrates**.

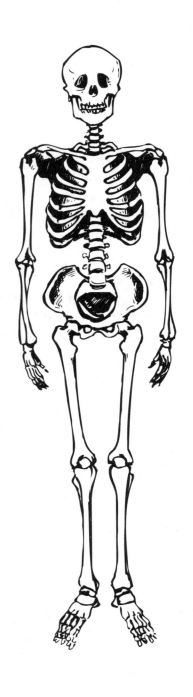

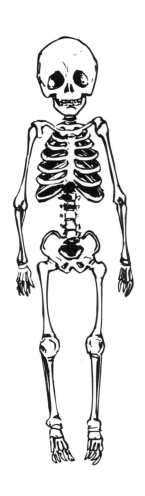

● Label the **ribs**, **spine**, **skull**, **femur**, **pelvis** and **breast bone** on these skeletons.

● Compare the bone in your forearm with that of a friend. Compare it with an adult's arm. What do you notice? What happens to your skeleton as you get older?

Vertebrates

● Look at this animal's teeth. (It is a plant eater.)

● Look at the size and position of its eye sockets. (It has very good vision.)

● Look at the long slender legs. (It moves at high speed.)

● What is it? _____

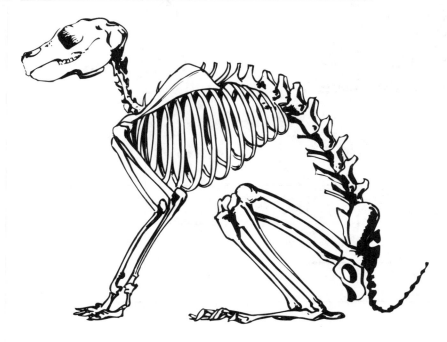

● Identify this vertebrate. Look closely for clues.

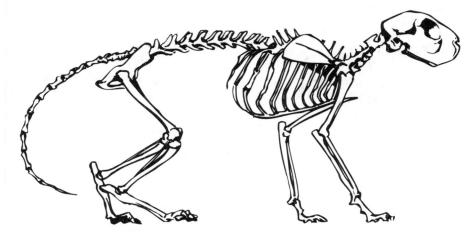

_____

● Compare the skeletons on this sheet with a human skeleton. What is different? What is the same?

_____

_____

_____

Animals without bony skeletons

Identify each of these creatures and say how the body is supported.

_____   _____

_____   _____

_____   _____

_____   _____

_____   _____

_____   _____

This group of animals is known as **invertebrates**.

Muscles and movement

Muscles are parts of the body that make things move. They are attached to bones by **tendons** – long, flexible cables.

● Feel your muscles when….

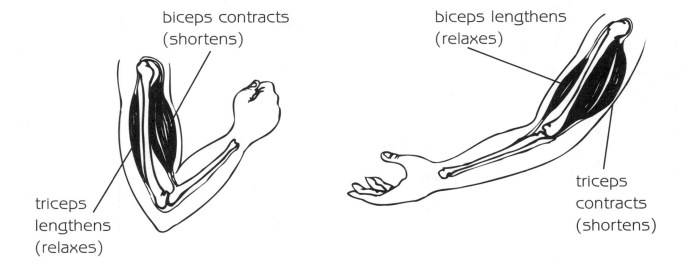

biceps contracts
(shortens)

triceps
lengthens
(relaxes)

… you **bend** your arm.

biceps lengthens
(relaxes)

triceps
contracts
(shortens)

…**unbend** your arm.

Muscles can't push so they work **in pairs**.

● Try making this.

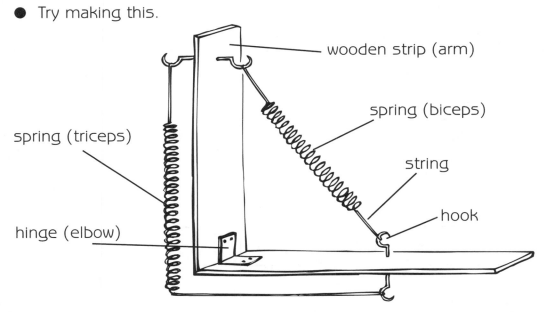

wooden strip (arm)

spring (biceps)

string

hook

spring (triceps)

hinge (elbow)

● The springs are your muscles. What happens to them when the wooden arm is raised and lowered?

Organisms

The plants and animals below are all **living things** or **organisms**.
Can you write their names in the correct group?

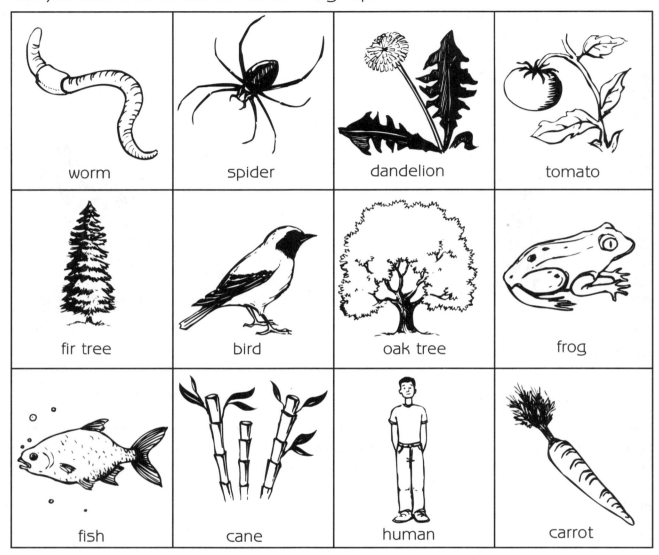

worm	spider	dandelion	tomato
fir tree	bird	oak tree	frog
fish	cane	human	carrot

Plants   **Animals**

_____   _____

_____   _____

_____   _____

_____   _____

_____   _____

_____   _____

Habitats

Plants and animals are found in different types of places called **habitats**. They live there because the **habitat** provides them with sufficient water, food, warmth and oxygen to survive.

● Draw a plant or animal that can be found in each of these habitats. (Draw each one in the blank space next to the habitat.)

● Can you think of another habitat? Draw it on the back of this sheet. Add a plant or animal that might live there.

Identification keys

● Use the key to identify **1**, **2** and **3**.

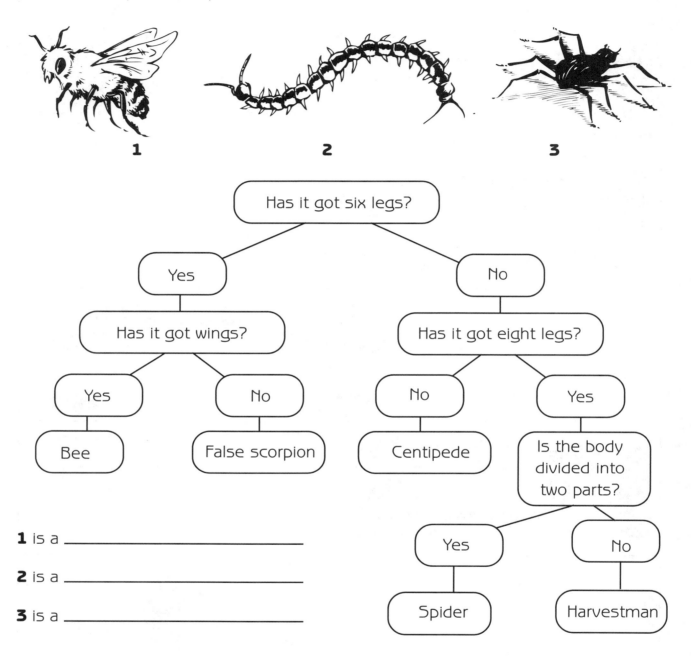

1   **2**   **3**

Has it got six legs?

Yes   No

Has it got wings?   Has it got eight legs?

Yes   No   No   Yes

Bee   False scorpion   Centipede   Is the body divided into two parts?

Yes   No

Spider   Harvestman

1 is a _____

2 is a _____

3 is a _____

● Can you write a key to help your friend identify these two birds?

goose   blackbird

Food chains

> Slugs can eat lettuces.   Kestrels can eat frogs.   Frogs can eat slugs.

Most food chains start with a **green plant**. Here the lettuce provides the energy (food) for the slug. The lettuce is the **producer** in this food chain. Each link eats the one before.

● Write and illustrate this food chain.

> Worms can eat leaves.
> Cats can eat birds.
> Birds can eat worms.

● Name the **producer** in this food chain. _____

Thermometers

● These thermometers have different uses, which is why they look different from each other. Find out what they are called.

● Can you suggest what they might be used for?

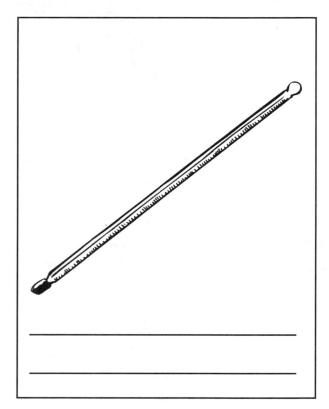

_____

_____

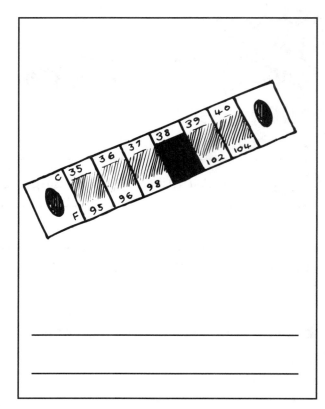

_____

_____

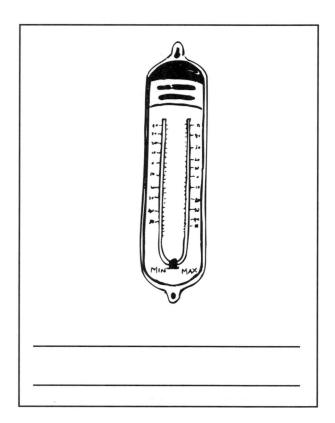

_____

_____

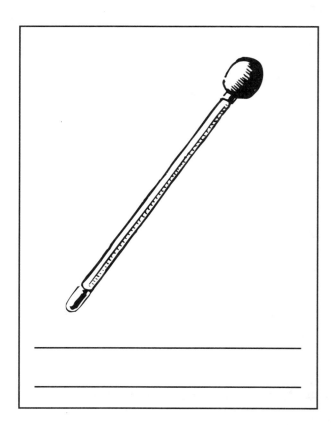

_____

_____

Wrap up!

● How could you find out which is the best material for keeping a cold drink cold, once it has been taken out of the fridge? Choose from the pictures below.

newspaper   bubble wrap   polythene

aluminium foil   sponge sheeting

For my test I will need _____

_____

I will _____

_____

_____

● Check: Is your test fair?
● With your teacher's help, carry out your test.

Keeping solids and liquids apart

● Are these **solids** or **liquids**? Put **L** or **S** in the boxes.

car oil ☐	sponge ☐	milk ☐	chocolate ☐	cola ☐
tea ☐	chair ☐	jelly ☐	rice ☐	ice cream ☐
shampoo ☐	cotton wool ☐	hair spray ☐	cooking oil ☐	salt ☐

● How are solids and liquids different from each other? What shape are they? Can you pour them? Can you spill them? Write some of your ideas in this table.

properties of solids	properties of liquids

Freezing, solidifying or melting

● Write above each arrow what has happened. The first one is done for you.

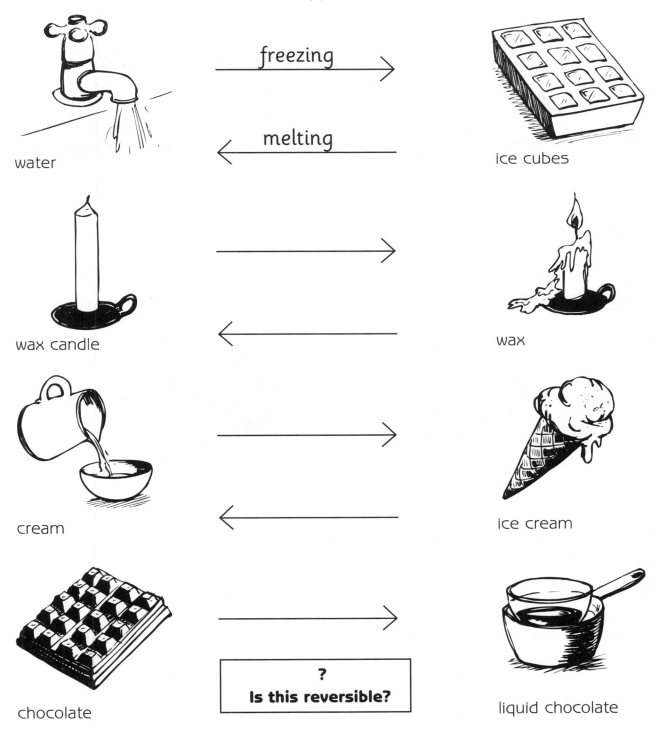

water   *freezing* →   ← *melting*   ice cubes

wax candle   wax

cream   ice cream

chocolate   **?
Is this reversible?**   liquid chocolate

● Complete these sentences.

A liquid can be changed into a solid by cooling and this is called

_____ or _____ .

A solid can be changed into a liquid by heating and this is _____ .

📖 S C H O L A S T I C

Separate (1)

● Make a mixture from these:

sand   rice   paper clips   dried peas

● Can you separate them?
Here are some ideas of what you might need:

colander   sieve

● Can you think of other ways to separate the materials?
Write down what you could do.

_____

_____

_____

_____

_____

_____

_____

What happens when?

● Draw what happens when you mix water with these materials.

 +  =

 +  =

 +  =

 +  =

● Can you explain what happens?
● Repeat with powder paint, chalk, sand, marbles and plaster of Paris.
● Record your results in a table.

Separate (2)

● Make a mixture of sand and water.
● Try to separate the sand from the water by **filtering**. Make filters from these things.

muslin   paper towels   gauze bandage   blotting paper

tea bags   coffee filters   fabrics

● Explain what happened in your experiment.

_____

_____

_____

_____

_____

_____

● Can you separate a solution of salt and water or sugar and water in the same way?

_____

_____

Friction

Friction is the force between two things rubbing together.
Friction usually makes things hot. Rub your hands together!

Complete the table with some ideas of your own.

High friction	Low friction
car tyres	skating
bicyle tyres	sliding
goalkeeper's gloves	
tying shoe laces	

SCHOLASTIC   83

Friction and forcemeters

● Read the forcemeter...

...when your friend pulls on it ☐ newtons

...when you pull open a drawer ☐ newtons

...when you drag an object across the floor. ☐ newtons

● On what kind of surface do objects slide more easily?

_____

● Test three different surfaces, for example wood, vinyl, carpet. Choose two more surfaces. Carry out a fair test and record your results on this bar chart.

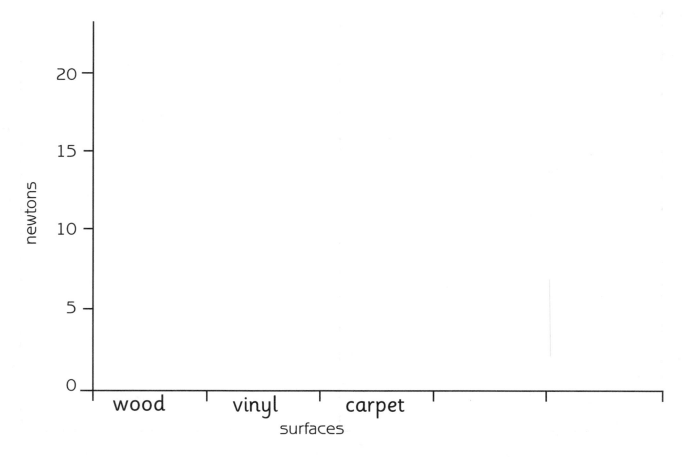

Good conductors

> Materials that electricity will flow through are called **conductors**.
> Materials that electricity cannot flow through are called **insulators**.

● Use a circuit like this to see which materials are best for conducting electricity. Try bridging the gap with these materials.

● Which materials make the bulb light up?
● What else can you test? Fill in this chart.

conductors	insulators

Making and breaking

A **circuit** must be complete for a device to work.

● Which **two corners** must be touched with the wires to complete this circuit and make the bulb light? _____

● Make a puzzle like this for a friend to try.

● A **switch** is a device for breaking a circuit. Why do we need switches?

_____

_____

_____

_____

HISTORY

In selecting worksheets for Year 4, we have broadly followed the content selected by the QCA in their *Scheme of Work for history*, thus we have sheets on the Tudors, the Second World War and the Ancient Egyptians. You might wish to note that the QCA allocate (depending on choices) between 30 and 54 hours to history. We have had to bear in mind that the Year 4 topics may actually be taught to different junior year groups, so the tasks are set down in such a way that they can be adapted for both the youngest and the oldest children. What we have provided is a compilation of historical sources and resources that can be used flexibly according to your needs.

Because six into four doesn't go precisely, apportioning the content of the history National Curriculum for Key Stage 2 is open to considerable variation. The six units – a local history study, three British history studies (Romans, Anglo-Saxons and Vikings in Britain; Britain and the wider world in Tudor times; and Victorian Britain *or* Britain since 1930), a European history study (Ancient Greece) and a world history study – do not even have to be taught separately. A local study might also focus on an area in Tudor times, a study of education in the locality might encompass Victorian Britain and Britain since 1930. But in practice the number of curriculum variations adopted by schools has tended to be quite small, the most common pathway through the historical maze being the broadly chronological one, with Ancient Egypt the most popular world history study. This is the path that we have followed here, although we clearly could not include sheets to service all possible local history projects.

There is a little background historical information in these notes but you are advised to refer to other reference material for more detail. There are plenty of books available. For succinct overviews of the historical topics for Key Stage 2, see: *History* in Scholastic's *Pocket Guides to the Primary Curriculum* series.

Who was Henry VIII? (page 91)

Objective: To identify features and characteristics of Henry VIII from a portrait.

What to do: Make sure that children have read and understood the sheet. They should then study the portrait for clues as to Henry's standing and character. It is a good idea to introduce the sheet by getting the class to compile a list of questions about the King's appearance. You might act as scribe and write them on the board or flip chart for all to see. Children then interrogate the picture on their own and complete the sentences that have been left unfinished. Excellent

guidance on interrogating portraits can be gleaned from *A teacher's guide to using portraits* by Susan Morris (English Heritage; ISBN 1-850-74231-6).

Differentiation: Less able children could work in a group, with an adult, to think of single words that describe Henry in this portrait, for example *stern, rich, important, solemn, dignified*, and so on. This should help them to tackle the assignment.

Extension: Children need to have a more rounded view of the King, so you might read them descriptions of him made by contemporaries, although the sources may not be readily understood without modification. Challenge children to find out four facts about Henry and to put them in order of importance. This would make a good homework task. Discuss the findings as a whole class. The results could be collated into a dossier titled 'Facts about Henry VIII'.

Henry's queens (page 92)

Objective: To know and use the names of the six wives of Henry VIII and to put them in order.

What to do: The cut-and-stick activity should be prefaced by the learning of the mnemonic – *Divorced, beheaded, died; Divorced, beheaded, survived.* Let children chant and cherish it – they will never forget it. The apparently tricky matching exercise is not so difficult if you use the dates as clues and start with the easiest ones, for example Jane Seymour 'died'

so, as the only one who dies, she clearly fits in the third top space 'Died 1537'.

Differentiation: Let less able children look beyond the sheet for help. Make sure that you have plenty of useful reference books, CD-ROMs and so on to support this work.

Extension: Challenge children to ask the question *Why did Henry VIII marry?* More able children might try to answer this with reference to each individual wife, although the underlying cause of his drive to marry needs to be established too.

Henry VIII: did and didn't (page 93)

Objective: To learn about the role and duties of a Tudor king.

What to do: It is worth studying the picture of King Henry VIII. Ask: *Where is he? Why is he surrounded by people? Who are they?* Children need to understand that the king had powers and duties and was always surrounded by courtiers. When they sort out the sentences (they may cut them out if you wish) they will find that the king did most of these things, except *did housework*, *did gardening* and *bought and sold things*. In fact, he did not do anything mundane. He did attend church regularly, as you would expect as head of the church; he played sport as a young man (tennis, for example), and had a reputation for music composition that, though true, has been exaggerated.

Differentiation: Cutting out the statements and handling them one at a time makes the sorting task a little more manageable for less able children. Once again it is important that children can refer to books and other reference material to help them to establish facts.

Extension: Children can investigate the role of a Tudor king still further using reference material. Can they find pictures that show Henry 'in action'? Can they find any other proof that he did the things that are listed? Compare with a modern monarch. Ask the children to find out three things that the current monarch does (a homework opportunity).

A comfortable house (page 94)

Objective: To identify features of some Tudor buildings.

What to do: Cutting out the picture, remounting it and then adding the labels, will give children more space to manoeuvre in and will help them to see more clearly how the building was constructed. The answers should be evident to teachers if not to children. What is not so self-evident is that Tudor houses, like modern houses, were not all identical and there was a big difference between a 'well-to-do' residence, a poor person's house and a wealthy person's stately home. There were also local differences in construction that emanated from the requirement to use local materials. Transporting large quantities of stone great distances cross-country would, for example, have been impossible. Make sure that ample reference material is available to enable children to complete the last task on the sheet.

Differentiation: Less able children would benefit from working in pairs on the first task. For the estate agent's description they will not only need reference material about Tudor houses, but may need to be shown what a modern estate agent's advertisement is like. A local newspaper is a useful resource.

Extension: A visit to a Tudor house would be an excellent follow up. There may be one locally. The Weald and Downland Museum near Chichester (www.wealddown.co.uk) has a collection of houses although they are bereft of interior furnishings and fittings. Constructing a model Tudor house based on the picture is a perfectly valid exercise provided children strive for accuracy in terms of dimensions and construction. You can construct the 'frame' of such a model just like the original, using prepared lengths of wood.

A list of clues (page 95)

Objective: To use documentary evidence (in this case a will) to draw inferences about the way some Tudor people lived.

What to do: The text of this document has been edited as little as possible so it will pose reading problems. This has been done deliberately so that children can realise the problems faced by historians when dealing with old documents – and this one is fairly recent and in English! This is a genuine will from 1592 and children will need to act as detectives to solve the problems it poses. In studying the will and making the lists as directed, children will gain an insight into the lives and possessions of Tudor people. *What items had a great deal of value in those days? Why?*

Differentiation: Any children initially stumped by this document need to be taken through it by an adult, one step at a time. First get children to underline any words that they do not understand (some spellings vary). Make it clear that you do not have the 'right' answers in an answer book and that you will have to work together to come up with 'best guesses'. Write in the meanings where required and then move on to tackling the set assignment.

Extension: Ask the children to list all the facts about life in Tudor times that they have learned from the will. You might wish to introduce the terms 'reliable' and 'authentic' to more able children. How does this will stand up in terms of reliability and authenticity?

The Second World War (page 96)

Objective: To understand when and where the war took place and why it was called a 'world' war.

What to do: When any historical topic is being studied in school, you can assume that children will already have some prior knowledge. It is a fact that we pick up much of our historical knowledge from sources outside school, so you could use this sheet as a way of establishing what that prior knowledge is. Alternatively, you might use it at the end of a topic you have studied in class to test what knowledge has been gained. If you allocate particular theatres of conflict to groups of children and then get them to report back to the whole class you will have a sharing of knowledge that will help all the class to gain some understanding of the war's key events. However this is tackled, there should be a plenary session where knowledge can be shared and the issues discussed.

Differentiation: Back-up and support in the form of books and other reference sources are essential when attempting this sheet. The Internet, CD-ROMs and encyclopedias could be very useful for tracking down facts about specific places and events as children's histories tend to deal with the war in broad brush strokes. Less able children should not struggle alone on this topic and this is an ideal assignment for giving to mixed-ability groups.

Extension: Compile a gazetteer of the Second World War. Let all the groups contribute by producing entries on several events in the war. Alternatively, get children to communicate their knowledge in another way, such as writing a newspaper report of one of the events; an interview with one of the combatants; or a battle report from one of the field commanders.

World War II timeline (page 97)

Objective: To know the key events and dates of the Second World War.

What to do: This is straightforward if the instructions on the sheet are followed. The dates make placing the events in order a simple matter assuming the class can cope with the numbers involved. The assignment should not end here: before children stick and illustrate as instructed on the sheet you should introduce activities that help them to remember the main events. They could be required to find out one more fact about each event listed, for example. Fold the dates out of sight and get the children to practise putting the events in time order without looking at them. (You might wish to cut them off entirely.)

Differentiation: Plenty of reference material must be available to support those that need it. The activity is easier if done at the end of a study of the war when children will be more familiar with the events on the timeline, although the more historically aware may well be able to tackle this sooner.

Extension: Get children to match these facts with a world map (they need to understand why it is known as a world war) so that they can learn both what and where. Challenge them to find out (say four facts) about one of the leaders during the war (Stalin, Hitler, Mussolini, Hirohito, Roosevelt, Churchill). This would make a good homework assignment.

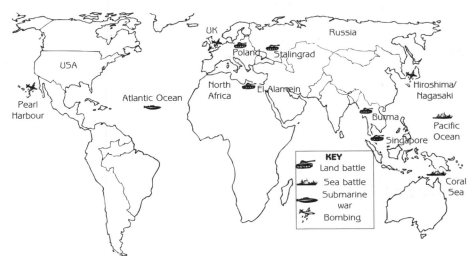

Evacuation (page 98)

Objective: To understand why the strategy of evacuation was used to protect children in the Second World War.

What to do: Over the primary years children should become familiar with the techniques required to deal with evidence. The poster on the sheet is a reproduction of a real piece of documentary evidence and children should approach it as such, interrogating it for clues. *What is it? Where did it come from? Why was it made? Who made it? Did it work?* You will need to introduce children to the term *evacuees*. If children are to design a poster of their own you will need to provide them with enough pictorial evidence for them to draw objects and people from the period in a fairly accurate way. Watch out for anachronisms in their art (no children in jeans on their mobile phones).

The government began to lay plans for the evacuation of children, the elderly and the disabled from industrial cities and ports early in the 1930s. In September 1938 (at the time of Munich) the plans included dividing up the country into three types of area: evacuation, neutral and reception. In August 1939 children returned to school early from the summer holiday in order to practise evacuation procedures. A government leaflet suggested that each child carry a handbag or case containing a gas mask, a change of underclothing, night clothes, house shoes or plimsolls, spare socks, a toothbrush, comb, towel, soap, face cloth, handkerchiefs and a warm coat or mackintosh. Evacuation plans were put into operation on the last day of August 1939 and in four days 1.9 million people were evacuated, including 1.5 million children.

Differentiation: This activity will mainly be differentiated by outcome although you may give some children the support of working with a partner on this assignment.

Extension: Investigate evacuation in your area. Which type of area was it? With a little local history research (there is usually a local group that will be only too pleased to help) you can find out about evacuation in your area. Some schools have successfully established links with areas to which children from their school were evacuated during the war. You may even have the great-grandchildren of evacuees in your school. Prepare a mock evacuee's bag (you may be able to borrow a real gas mask).

Ancient Egypt: model behaviour
(page 99)

Objective: To make inferences and deductions from objects.

What to do: Any reasonable interrogation of this piece of evidence should enable the children to label the pictures correctly, although children should understand that the objects did not come 'labelled' and so even the 'right' answers are no more than informed guesses.

The funerary sculptures shown here are made of wood, carved and painted, and were part of a set found on top of the coffin of a provincial governor who had been buried in a cave at Beni Hasa, a cliff face on the east bank of the Nile.

Differentiation: Less able children should tackle this sheet in a supportive group.

Extension: Let children replicate the models using clay or soft wood. They could then describe in detail how the Ancient Egyptians carried out these tasks. They could pretend that their models were in a museum and write the display labels for them.

Land of the Nile (page 100)

Objectives: To locate Ancient Egypt on a historical map; to learn its main geographical features.

What to do: This is a good 'end-of-project' assignment as it tests the information that children have acquired. From the text on the sheet alone it should be possible for most children to annotate and colour the map correctly.

Differentiation: Reference books, maps and pictures are essential to give support to less able children for this assignment and should be displayed as part of the project in any case. More able children should be expected to complete the task without resorting to books. Once again the task is eased if it is undertaken collectively – children can work in pairs or in small groups.

Extension: Collect pictures of Egypt (travel brochures are useful) and display them. From maps and pictures challenge children to make deductions about what life in ancient Egypt might have been like. What might be the good/bad aspects of life in ancient Egypt? Children might also design a travel brochure for a modern visitor to the ancient historic sites of the Nile. Where would they visit? What would they see there?

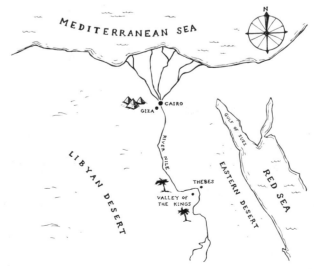

Who was Henry VIII?

Henry VIII became king of England nearly 500 years ago. He ruled from 1509 to 1547. He was the eighth king with the name Henry so he was known as Henry the eighth. (In Roman numerals V=5 III=3, so VIII=8.) He belonged to the Tudor family and the Tudor rose, which was both red and white, was its symbol.

King Henry VIII by Hans the Younger Holbein (1497/8–1543), Thyssen-Bornemisza Collection, Madrid, Spain/Bridgeman Art Library

● Study his portrait carefully. What does the picture tell you about Henry? Finish the sentences below.

I think that Henry was

_____

_____

_____

I think this because

_____

_____

_____

I also think that Henry was

_____

_____

_____

I think this because

_____

_____

_____

● Use reference books to help you colour in the rose.

Henry's queens

Henry VIII had six wives. This rhyme tells what happened to them – in order.

> Divorced, beheaded, died.
> Divorced, beheaded, survived.

● Cut out the portraits of the queens and stick them in the correct places.

divorced (1533)	beheaded (1536)	died (1537)

divorced (1540)	beheaded (1542)	survived Henry VIII

Anne of Cleves. Married in 1540. Only married for a few months.

Catherine Howard. Married in 1540.

Jane Seymour. Married in 1536. Died after her son Edward was born.

Catherine of Aragon. Married in 1509. Had a daughter Mary.

Catherine Parr. Married in 1543. Clever and well-educated, she outlived the King.

Anne Boleyn. Married in 1533. Had a daughter Elizabeth.

Henry VIII: did and didn't

● What did King Henry VIII actually do? Sort these sentences into two groups, **Did** and **Didn't**.

He met ambassadors from other countries.
He talked with advisors about money and other business.
He did housework.
He led the army into battle.
He went hunting.
He did gardening.
He wrote and played music.
He went to church regularly.
He played sport.
He attended grand banquets.
He signed government papers and laws.
He bought and sold things.

A comfortable house

The houses of poor people who lived in Tudor times were so badly built that they did not last long. Most of the Tudor houses that survive today were built by people who were comfortably off – farmers, merchants and professional people such as lawyers.

● Fit these labels correctly.

> oak framework

> brick chimney

> window bars (no glass panes – shutters were used at night)

> brick in-fill between timbers

> wattle and daub in-fill (woven hazel twigs plastered over with a mixture of dung, clay, lime and straw)

● Find out more about Tudor houses.
● Write an estate agent's description of this house as if you were trying to sell it.

A list of clues

We can learn a great deal about what it was like in Tudor times from documents that have survived. Inventories (lists of house contents) and wills tell us what people owned and valued.

This is part of Isabel Watkinson's will (1492). Read it carefully. What do you notice about the spelling? Make a list of the things she gave away. Who did she give them to?

In the name of God, amen.
I Isabell Watkinson, of good health and perfecte remembrance but sycke in body, do make this laste will and testamente.

I bequeathe my soule to almighty God my maker and to Jesus Christ his Son my Savioure and Redeemer and my bodye to be buried in the paryshe churche of Heath.

Item: I give and bequeathe to my son Rycharde all my corn in the folde and all my croppe of corne in my barne savinge that he shall give to Humphrey my son half a quarter of harderaine.

Item: I give also to my son Rycharde my beste potte and my best panne.

Item: I give and bequeathe unto Humphrey my said sone my beste potte and my beste panne next and all the rest of my brasse to be equally divided amongste all my children generallye, both sonse and daughters.

Item: I give and bequeathe to Rycharde my said sone three of my beste dublers.

Item: I give and bequeathe to Rycharde my said sone two of my beste cattell, the cattell remaynest to my other children, everyone of them.

Item: I give and bequeathe to Mary Bakon a ringed heffer about two years olde.

Item: I give and bequeathe to Rycharde my said sone one ffether bedde and a boulster and the coverlytt which ye yet arranged to make – a new coverlytt.

Item: I gyve to my sons Robert Watkinson's children everyone of them, 12 pence.

Item: I give and bequeathe unto my three daughters, Jane, Agnes and Alice, all my apparyll and all my apparyll wayre in my cheste which dost stand by my bedde heade.

Item: I wyll that Robert Watkinson's childe to my sone Robert Watkinson shall have the counter table in the house and a share in two great chests in the boultinge house.

Item: I give and bequeathe unto Humphrey my said sone two shepe. And all the rest of the shepe I give to Rycharde my sone.

Item: I give and bequeathe to William Harryson my servante two yards of empon cloth to make him a shirt.

I the sayd Isabell Watkinson have to this laste wyll and testamente sett my hand and marke.

The Second World War

This map shows some of the events of the Second World War. Why was it called a 'world' war? Choose one of the places shown on the map and write a paragraph about what happened there. You will have to do some research like a historian!

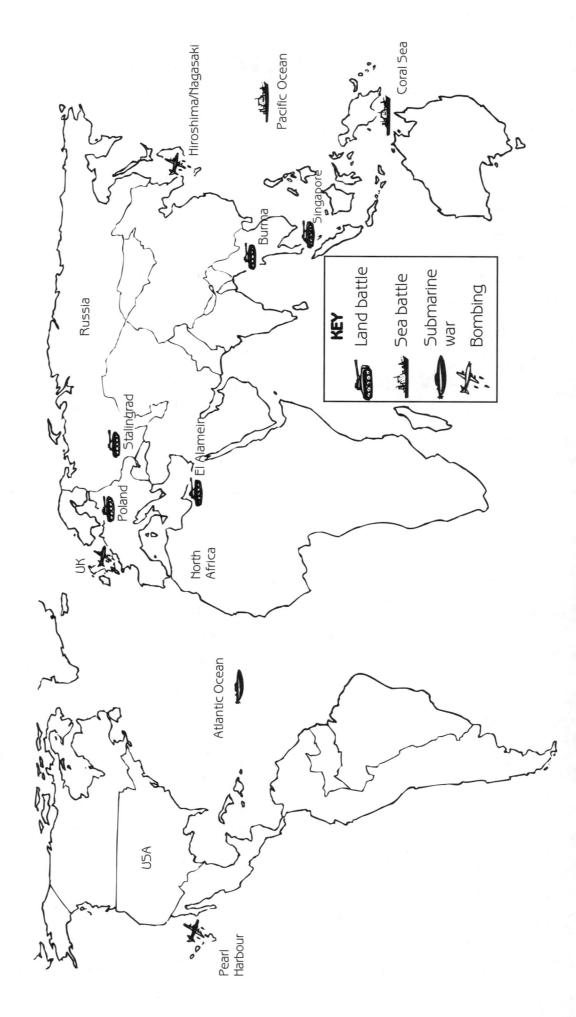

KEY

Land battle

Sea battle

Submarine war

Bombing

Hiroshima/Nagasaki

Pacific Ocean

Coral Sea

Singapore

Burma

Russia

Stalingrad

El Alamein

Poland

North Africa

UK

Atlantic Ocean

USA

Pearl Harbour

World War II timeline

Cut out these strips. Arrange them in the correct time order. Stick them on a large sheet of paper and illustrate the timeline. Add more detailed information.

1942	The British defeat the German and Italian armies at El Alamein.
1944	The Allies land an army in Normandy in order to recapture Europe from the Germans.
1939	The first evacuation of children from cities begins in Britain.
1941	Without warning the Japanese bomb the Americans at Pearl Harbour.
1940	Winston Churchill becomes Prime Minister.
1945	Germany surrenders.
1943	The Russians defeat the Germans in the battle for the city of Stalingrad.
1945	USA drops atomic bombs on the Japanese cities of Hiroshima and Nagasaki. Japan surrenders. The Second World War ends.
1940	German airforce begins heavy bombing of London and other British cities.

■SCHOLASTIC   97

Evacuation

● Look carefully at this poster. What is it trying to persuade people to do? Why?
● What was the Ministry of Health Evacuation Scheme? Who was it for? Why only them?

● Design a poster of your own to try to get people to join the scheme.

Ancient Egypt: model behaviour

- These wooden carvings were found in caves on the bank of the river Nile in Egypt. Look carefully. What do they tell us about life in Ancient Egypt?

- Can you find and label: a man and woman pounding dough, a brewer soaking barley for beer making, a water carrier lifting jars of water, a woman rolling grain to make flour?

Model of servants making bread and brewing, Egyptian, early XII Dynasty, 1963–1862BC (painted wood, linen and clay). Fitzwilliam Musuem, University of Cambridge, UK/Bridgeman Art Library.

Land of the Nile

The Ancient Egyptians needed the river Nile. It flooded to give them fertile soil on which to grow crops.

The Nile delta (where the river spread out to meet the sea in the north) was fertile land. This was called Lower Egypt. The narrow valley of the river was called Upper Egypt.

Egypt is surrounded by desert (known as the Red Land) where Egyptians hunted and found stone for building. The pyramids were built on the edge of the desert because fertile soil (the Black Land) was too precious for building on.

The Nile is 4187 miles long, the longest river in the world. About 60 million people live in Egypt today, in ancient times it was probably only 3 million.

Colour and label this map using the facts you have learned.

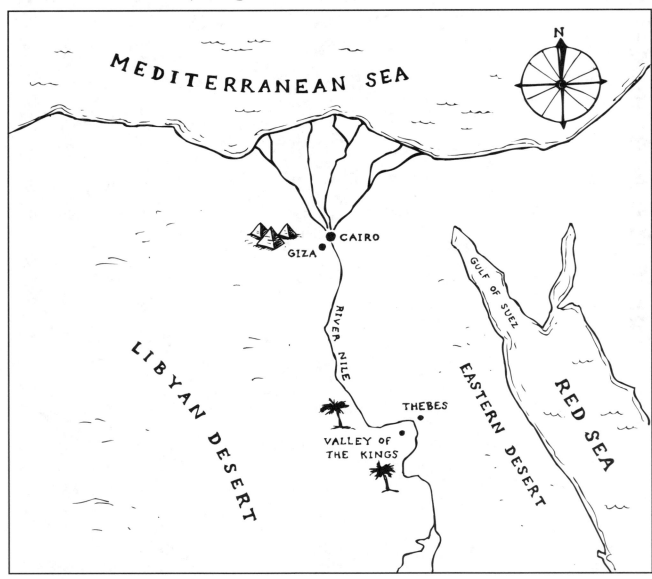

GEOGRAPHY

The old saying about geography being concerned with 'maps' begins to look more apposite as children move to the Year 4 geography curriculum. Places and people from a wider world take a more central position in the curriculum. There are also curriculum choices for the teacher to make and as we cannot guess what those might be, we have gone with the suggestions in the QCA Scheme of Work for geography, hence the references to India in our sheets. Your choice of place may legitimately be different. Two of the sheets cover the relationship between children's leisure, recreation and working time – links dealt with in one of the QCA's optional additional units (Unit 19).

Children's progressive geographical development, in the four areas defined by the National Curriculum (geographical enquiry and skills; knowledge and understanding of places; knowledge and understanding of patterns and processes; knowledge and understanding of environmental change and sustainable development) takes place through the topics set down in the 'breadth of study' section of the National Curriculum's Programme of Study. The QCA's geography Scheme of Work suggests three units of study to cover this with an estimated time allocation of between 28 and 47 hours – a substantial amount of teaching time. In addition, the QCA suggest an overarching unit for the entire key stage ('What's in the news?') to be dipped into during Key Stage 2. You might find it useful to refer to the QCA matrix of curriculum coverage (Revised appendix 4, pp16/17 Geography Teacher's Guide Update).

What a load of rubbish! (1)

(page 104)

Objectives: To become aware of the amount of waste within the classroom; to collect and record evidence relating to this issue.

What to do: Children should be familiar with handling data in the graphical form used on this sheet. This is a fieldwork assignment that involves the collection and recording of evidence in order to answer a specific question. The sheet does not contain a question – it is taken as read – but you should preface the use of the sheet by discussing the issues with the class. What environmental problems are there around the school? Issues such as noise, air pollution and waste may be discussed. How much waste is produced by the class each day? Remember to make sensible and safe provision for the handling of classroom waste material. You might weigh the waste in a bin and simply deduct the weight of the bin. The data can be recorded straight onto the graph. If you wish to have more evidence, the sheet can be duplicated and used to track waste over any period of time.

Differentiation: You may need to revise how to record data on a block graph with some children. Mixed-ability grouping is perhaps the best way to cope with differentiation for this activity.

Extension: Discussion may well yield additional or subsidiary questions to be answered. *How much of the waste that we throw away in the classroom could be recycled? How could this be organised? Is all our classroom waste necessary? How could we cut down on classroom waste?* A further activity might involve recording the amounts of different categories of waste such as packaging, cartons, food, discarded work and so on. With parental co-operation the photocopiable sheet could be used to record the weight of daily rubbish produced at home.

What a load of rubbish! (2)

(page 105)

Objectives: To collect and record evidence about the waste in the school grounds; to recognise how people affect their environment.

What to do: Be clear that this assignment is concerned with rubbish in the school grounds. Do not focus on the waste in the school's main bins which will contain large quantities of food waste and possible hazardous materials. Concentrate on litter and/or litter bins only. Even so you should only let children handle waste wearing protective gloves and under supervision. In most cases this is a perfectly safe and sensible assignment but you should use your judgement if you feel that the data collection is too hazardous (depending on what is frequently part of the school's litter.)

This task takes the previous activity 'What a load of rubbish! (1)' on one stage further in that it requires the sorting and weighing of rubbish. Once again, discussion of the issues should take place before the activity commences. What questions will the collection and recording of this data answer? Discuss how the different categories of rubbish could be recycled, for example in bottle banks, compost heaps.

Differentiation: As above, mixed-ability grouping is perhaps the best way to cope with differentiation for this activity.

Extension: Is there a need for improvement? Get children to recognise areas of the school grounds that could be improved. Which areas might benefit from additional bins, or the withdrawal of bins? Which areas are neglected? Challenge children to produce a plan for improving an area of the school grounds.

Settlements (page 106)

Objective: To use maps to obtain evidence about settlements.

What to do: By studying the map, children find places with the endings specified. The next phase requires some research but information on place name endings is readily available. (Most children's history books on the Viking and Saxon invasions contain information about place name endings.) The Viking endings mean: -by = farm/village; -ton = an enclosure or village; -thorpe = hamlet. You can change the selected endings if you wish to choose endings more frequently seen in your area. Children may notice other place name endings on the map, such as -wick (dwelling, specialised farm or trading settlement) and -holme (dry ground in a marsh). The children then answer the three questions for each of the villages they have chosen at the bottom of the sheet. This requires a close study of the map. Can the children recognise a river on a map? Can they read a map sufficiently to recognise flat land? From the evidence of the map can children suggest why settlements were started in these places?

Differentiation: If children are not sufficiently competent at reading an OS map you should undertake additional revision work. Use local 1:50 000 maps on which to pick out key features such as contours and rivers. As for the worksheet, you might enlarge the extract to facilitate the reading of the place names.

Extension: Consider a single place (the children's own village/town would be best)

and ask children to suggest at least two reasons why people might originally have settled there. Clearly the question is a geographical and historical one ('because it is close to the M1' will not do!) and is aimed at emphasising the fact that settlements developed as a result of a number of factors. This could be a homework task.

Where am I? (page 107)

Objective: To use four-figure grid references accurately.

What to do: This sheet uses four-figure references only, so children using the map will be directed to a square not a precise point. The exercise is only a beginning and children should then practise the use of map references further. Once their answers have been checked, children should begin working in pairs to test each other's skill. *Can you find what is in square 3294?* And so on.

Differentiation: 'Into the house before going up the stairs' is a good way of remembering how to read map references but this will need practising. Groups of children who find this difficult should play 'Tic-tac-toe' on a numbered grid. This can be done on the board with group A versus group B or noughts versus crosses.

Extension: Select two references on the map (two clearly identifiable features) and ask children to describe the route from one to the other. A possible homework task.

From Britain to India (page 108)

Objectives: To use and interpret a world map; to locate India and the UK.

What to do: The instructions are given on the sheet. Make sure that the children understand what they have to do before they begin the task. The final question is intended for open-ended discussion; definite answers are not essential. Let them discuss whether they would go over land or by air, and how they would do either.

Differentiation: Support should be provided in the form of atlases and globes. Even those children who work without the atlas support should be encouraged to compare their answers with the atlas. Make sure that the atlas is up-to-date and not too complicated. Does it indicate the boundary of Europe? Less able children can draw round the country outlines quite roughly.

Extension: Follow up by asking children to find out key data about India from an atlas. Which countries border it? Which seas border it? What main mountain ranges and rivers does India possess? Give children a blank outline map of India on which they can put this information. This could be a homework task.

An Indian market (page 109)

Objectives: To identify features of a place from a resource; to use that resource to identify similarities and differences between that place and the local area.

What to do: The photograph is of an Indian market in Calcutta. Get children to interrogate this source. You might choose to start this as a whole-class exercise first using an OHP. You will need to give children access to reference books that will provide the information that they require, so it is best to make this a group assignment in order to spread the strain on your resources.

Differentiation: Identifying the fruits and plants is not easy. Copy and reproduce reference pictures for distribution to those children who may have difficulty in finding the information for themselves.

Extension: Children will have made some comparisons between this market and a market they know when they first study the source. Set them the task of recording these points of comparison. *What things are the same? What things are different? What are the differences in displaying goods? Packaging goods? Paying for goods?* Visit a local market. Take photographs for comparison purposes.

How do you spend your time?

(page 110)

Objective: To distinguish between work, leisure and recreation.

What to do: Distinguish between the three categories and discuss the differences with the class. (Note that leisure time can be filled with activities that might be recreational. Recreation generally involves activity, physical effort and takes place outside the home. Leisure involves relaxation and may take place at home. All sport should be defined as recreation.) Having clarified the categories, children record examples of their work, leisure and recreation on the sheet.

Differentiation: Children can start by listing all the activities in which they take part and *then* sort them into categories. Less able children could record their answers pictorially but more able children should use both words and pictures.

Extension: Children can repeat this task for another person. They might interrogate Grandma or Dad or another amenable adult in the family.

How do you spend your time: a questionnaire (page 111)

Objective: To devise a questionnaire.

What to do: Devising a questionnaire is not an easy task. The best way to tackle this sheet is as a whole class. The categories should be clear in the children's minds (see previous activity, 'How do you spend your time?') but an example of each is given on the outline questionnaire. As a class, complete the lists started under *what?* and *where?* The children can then complete the questionnaire as individuals. You then need to collate all the data and get children to work out totals and averages.

Differentiation: Completing the sheet by ticking boxes should not prove to be too difficult for any child, but coping with the analysis and presentation of the data will be more difficult. For less able children, reduce the demands upon them by asking them to focus on one piece of data at a time, for example information relating to watching TV. You can then get them to tackle all the data bit by bit or limit the amount of data to be analysed. *How much time is spent by the class in total watching TV? What is the average time spent per week by each child?*

Extension: You may take the opportunity to use a suitable ICT software package to carry out the data analysis. Present the data graphically. You can handle the 'where?' data differently if you choose. Challenge children to mark the locations used for the various activities on a map of your area using a colour-coding system.

What a load of rubbish! (1)

Estimate, then weigh, your classroom rubbish each day and record your results.

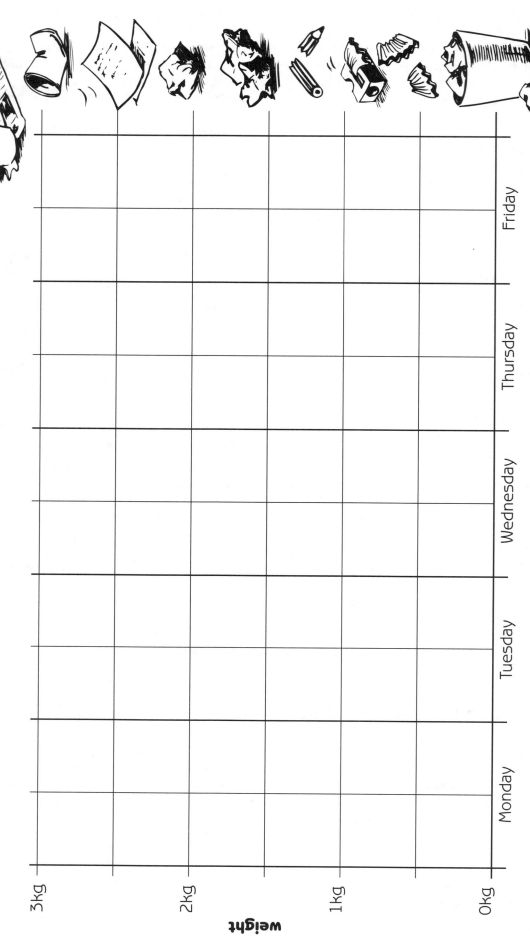

weight					
3kg					
2kg					
1kg					
0kg	Monday	Tuesday	Wednesday	Thursday	Friday

days of the week

What a load of rubbish! (2)

Sort and weigh the rubbish from your bins.

bin _____   day _____   total weight _____

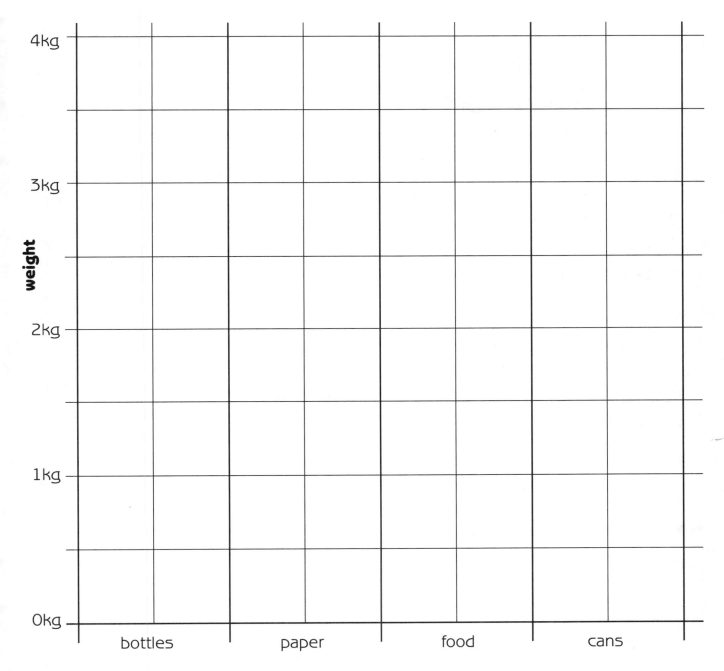

weight

4kg

3kg

2kg

1kg

0kg

bottles   paper   food   cans

rubbish

Settlements

● Look carefully at this section of an OS (ordnance survey) map.

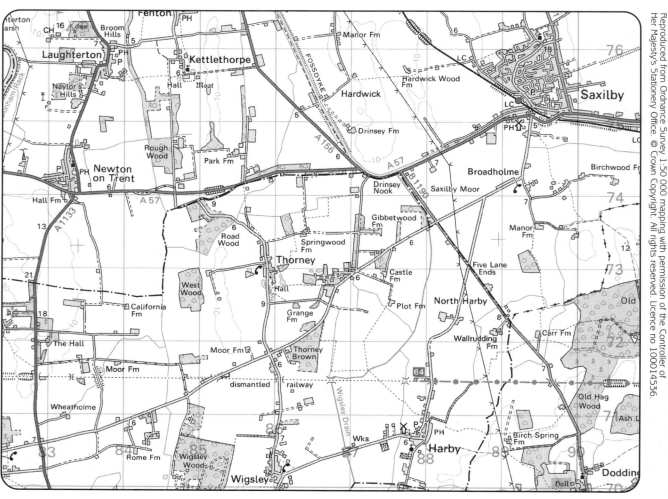

● Choose four villages/towns ending in -by, -ton and -thorpe.

1. _____   2. _____

3. _____   4. _____

● Find out what these endings mean. Write on the back of the sheet.

● Is the village/town on a river crossing?

1. _____   2. _____   3. _____   4. _____

● Is there flat land for farming?

1. _____   2. _____   3. _____   4. _____

● Is there any danger of flooding?

1. _____   2. _____   3. _____   4. _____

Where am I?

● On this map, Little Newbury is in square 3092. Find it.

30 (the number along the bottom)
92 (the number up the side)

Remember we go in the door

before going up the stairs.

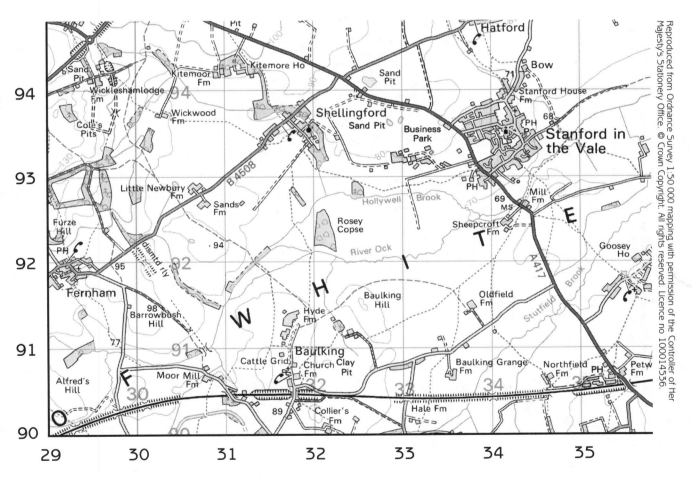

● What can you find in these squares on the map?

3493 _____

3292 _____

3093 _____

2990 _____

From Britain to India

- Find Britain. Draw round it in red.
- Find Asia. Draw round it in yellow.
- Find Europe. Draw round it in blue.
- Draw a key for your map.
- Find India. Draw round it in green.

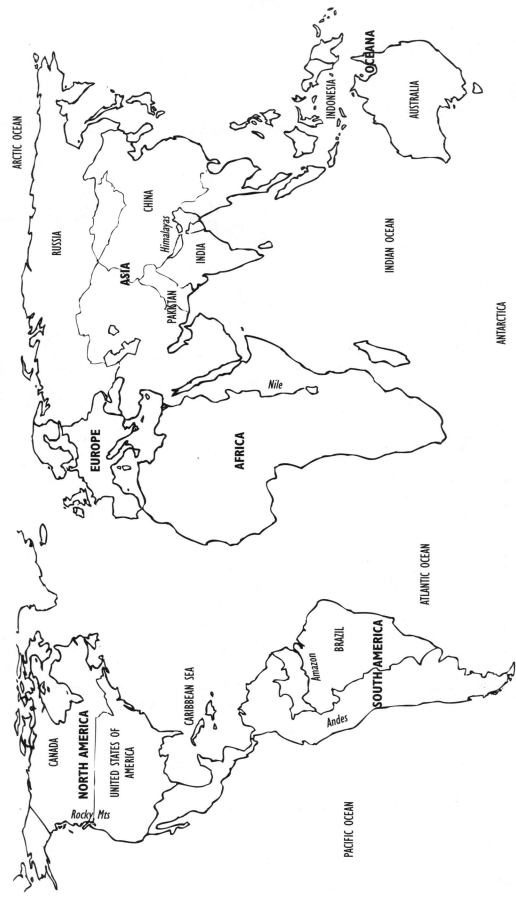

- Plan a route to India from Britain. How would you get there? Which countries would you cross? Which airports would you use?

An Indian market

© TRIP/H Rogers

- How can you tell it is hot?
- Why do people wear loose-fitting clothes?
- Find out about saris, dhotis and lungis.
- Compare this market with your local market.

- Identify these foods found in an Indian market. Would we eat them raw or cooked?

orange

cauliflower

aubergine

chilli

guava

coriander

ginger

SCHOLASTIC   **109**

How do you spend your time?

Fill in each category with as much information as you can.

work

reading

recreation

football

leisure

piano playing

How do you spend your time: a questionnaire

This questionnaire is not finished. Complete the questions and then hand a copy to each child in the class to fill in the data.

What?	Where?			How long? (per week)		
	home	school	other	2 hours or more	1 hour	½ hour or less
WORK housework ☐☐☐☐☐	☐☐☐☐☐	☐☐☐☐☐	☐☐☐☐☐	☐☐☐☐☐	☐☐☐☐☐	☐☐☐☐☐
LEISURE reading ☐☐☐☐☐	☐☐☐☐☐	☐☐☐☐☐	☐☐☐☐☐	☐☐☐☐☐	☐☐☐☐☐	☐☐☐☐☐
RECREATION skating ☐☐☐☐☐	☐☐☐☐☐	☐☐☐☐☐	☐☐☐☐☐	☐☐☐☐☐	☐☐☐☐☐	☐☐☐☐☐

DESIGN AND TECHNOLOGY

Design and technology in the National Curriculum is concerned with developing ideas – that is, planning, making products, and evaluating them. This can be done by (1) investigating familiar products, (2) practical tasks (for developing skills and techniques), and (3) designing and making products. Practical experience is the key to all learning in design and technology. The QCA suggest between 32 and 40 hours for Year 4 children. All schemes for design and technology must involve a great deal of designing and making so this element has been included in our activities here, which means that using them generally involves the need for materials and equipment, close supervision and appropriate health and safety precautions.

Money in materials (page 114)

Objective: To design a product using textiles for a specific purpose.

What to do: The first activity on the sheet is a matter of observation. Children should interrogate the pictures to arrive at their answers. Although this can be an individual task, it is recommended that children work in pairs. The aim is to get children to think carefully about types of containers that are used to hold money and the different ways in which they fasten. The answers are left open, as without handling the objects it is not possible to be definitive about the materials used, but one would expect leather, cloth and plastic to be included. Based upon these observations, the children then tackle the 'design-and-make' activity at the bottom of the sheet. This is best attempted after the children have had a chance to physically examine and pull apart some money containers. They need to understand that joining needs to be secure and strong, have some idea about size, and be clear about choice of material. They should draw up a list of design criteria before they begin (see the questions at the bottom of the sheet). NB: You will need to decide what materials and tools you are going to provide. For example, you could knit a container; are you going to include the materials for this option?

Differentiation: This should be a 'hands-on' activity for all children, but for less able children the provision of a range of purses to examine is essential. You might wish to reduce the demands made upon them by specifying for whom the purse is to be made, for example a very young child, a jogger, an elderly lady.

Extension: Ask the children to complete a glossary of relevant terms including clear definitions and suitable illustrations, for example strap, seam, hook, button, buckle, belt, press stud, zip, Velcro. They might also make an inventory of the range of money containers in their home, listing dimensions, fastening device and construction material. This could be a homework task.

Sew a seam (page 115)

Objective: To sew using a range of different stitches.

What to do: You will need to provide the needles, thread and fabric for this activity and make health and safety arrangements. How will you distribute, store and handle sewing needles? You need to be confident that, with your children, this activity does not carry undue risk. Children should use the sheet as a sewing instruction manual and do as directed.

Differentiation: Some children will be very demanding of adult assistance when undertaking this activity. A classroom assistant or other helper will be needed to support children who lack manipulative skills.

Extension: Test the strength of different methods of joining two pieces of fabric together. Give children the material and equipment to do this and allow them to experiment. *How can you test the joins fairly?*

Controlling comic clown (1) and (2)
(pages 116 and 117)

Objective: To investigate lever and linkage systems and to apply what they have learned.

What to do: This task should not be done in isolation, but set in the context of a study of linkage-type mechanisms. Children should have examined a range of products with moving parts (pop-up books, puppets, toy trains and so on) and attempted to explain how the moving parts are moved. During these examinations encourage use of technical vocabulary such as *lever, linkage, pivot*.

You should make the hair-raising clown shown on page 116 to demonstrate to the class. A good introduction is to tell a story about a clown that involves the raising of his hair, using the cardboard clown to illustrate it. Based upon their observations, the children then construct a clown of their own with a different moving part or parts using a similar simple lever device.

Children can use the template on page 117 for help in designing the basic structure so that they can concentrate on the creation of the lever mechanism.

Differentiation: It is hard to gauge how much help children will need with this activity, as they can vary enormously in dexterity and mechanical understanding. You may wish to provide ready-cut templates for some, whereas others will simply need the card, glue and scissors and a bit of encouragement. Outcomes will probably vary enormously, too. Extra adult help in the classroom is recommended.

Extension: As a culmination to this task, ask children to tell a story, using the comic clown to illustrate it.

Are you switched on? (1)

(page 118)

Objective: To understand the way in which different types of switches can be activated.

What to do: This sheet and the next are companion sheets, containing illustrations of switches that the children can either make for themselves or examine and explain.

Provide the usual wires and batteries that the children use for the construction of simple circuits. Make sure that you have the equipment required for the making of the two switches illustrated at the top of the sheet – card, drawing pins, paper clips, metal foil, small pieces of softwood blocks, wire. Children should examine and discuss the simple switches and replicate them. The trip switch is more complicated and the sheet simply asks that they explain how it works (the foil is connected to the carton and is pulled by the string when it is tripped, this makes a connection and completes the circuit setting off the alarm.) Let the children work in pairs. When they have agreed a satisfactory explanation, they should report to an adult.

Differentiation: Children, particularly those less able, must work co-operatively on this, although you might challenge a more able child to complete the task alone. Essentially teachers should keep a low profile once the activity is underway. Let children make mistakes and try a number of solutions. Adults should only intervene when frustration begins to set in with a vengeance. Children will learn by trial and success.

Extension: Challenge children to replicate the trip switch illustrated. (You will need to provide a small alarm and the other equipment illustrated.)

Are you switched on? (2)

(page 119)

Objective: To understand the way in which different types of switches can be activated.

What to do: Again, let the children work in pairs and discuss how they think the rain switch works. *What*

will trigger the alarm? Why is it called a rain switch? There is space for them to write down their ideas, if they wish. (It works because the water dissolves the sugar so the peg closes and the two drawing pins touch, completing the circuit, thus setting off the alarm!) It would be advantageous for children to do both this and the previous sheet although it is not essential. It would also be useful to let children examine and, if sensible and safe, to take apart some commercially produced switches to see how they function.

Differentiation: See above, 'Are you switched on? (1)'.

Extension: The next sheet, 'Alarming!', can also serve as a follow-up extension activity. Once again the extension activity challenge will be to replicate the switch illustrated on the sheet.

Alarming! (page 120)

Objective: To apply what they have learned about switches to constructing an alarm.

What to do: Understanding about switches, alarms and circuits is essential before children attempt this sheet. It is recommended that the two previous sheets be prerequisite for this one. One approach is to use the sheet as a focus for group or class discussion because children need to be clear what is required to trigger the alarm before they start to design and make one. Refer them to the switches that they examined previously. The essential equipment required is listed on the sheet although you might wish to provide more than this.

Differentiation: Support can be provided by: adult intervention (have a classroom assistant on standby); illustrative material such as information books that show pictorially various simple circuits and alarms; and ready-made alarm circuits exemplifying the principles shown on the previous two sheets.

Extension: Ask children to use a control box and computer program to make their alarm work. This kind of application of ICT to D&T is included in the National Curriculum. If you are unfamiliar with this technology then consult your co-ordinator.

Money in materials

● Look at these money containers. What materials do you think they are made from? Why?

● Label the following on the drawings above:

(seam)   (strap)   (hem)   (press stud)

(zip)   (Velcro)   (buckle)   (button)

● How do they fasten? Can you think of any other fasteners?

● Design and make a purse or wallet.
  ● Who will use it?
  ● What material will it be made from?
  ● How will it fasten?

Sew a seam

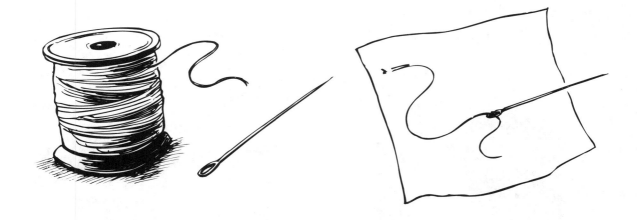

● Start and finish on the wrong side of the material by making a few stitches on top of each other. Practise these stitches:

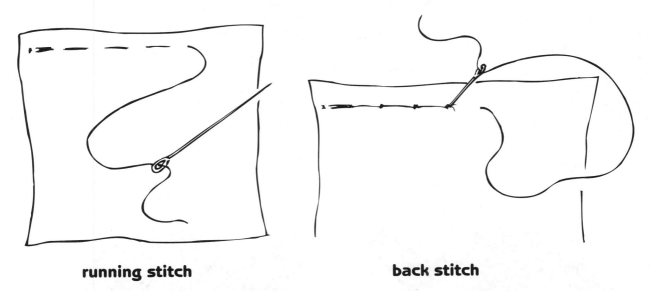

running stitch

back stitch

● Which is the strongest joining stitch? Investigate:

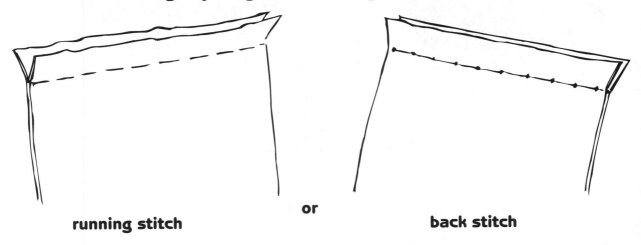

running stitch

or

back stitch

● In what other ways can we join two pieces of material together? Investigate.

Controlling comic clown (1)

Hair-raising!

● Explain to a friend how the clown's hair is raised.

slides up and
down

● Now it's your turn. Make the clown's head from stiff card and use card strips and paper fasteners to make his eyes, nose or ears move.

Controlling comic clown (2)

Are you switched on? (1)

- Can you see how these two **pressure switches** work?
- Can you make a similar **pressure switch** but use foil?

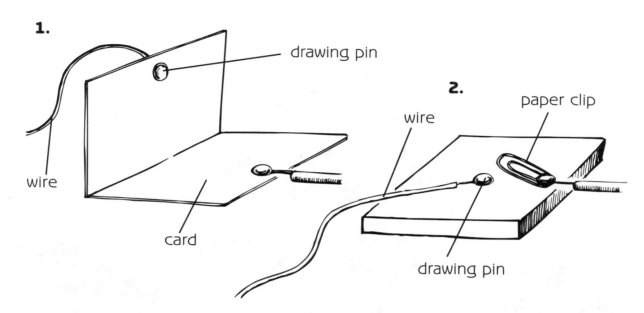

1.

drawing pin

wire

card

2.

wire

paper clip

drawing pin

- How do you think this **trip switch** works?

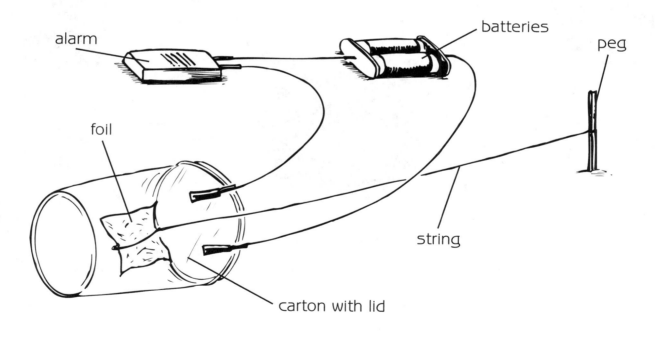

alarm

batteries

peg

foil

string

carton with lid

_____

_____

_____

_____

Are you switched on? (2)

How do you think this **rain switch** works?

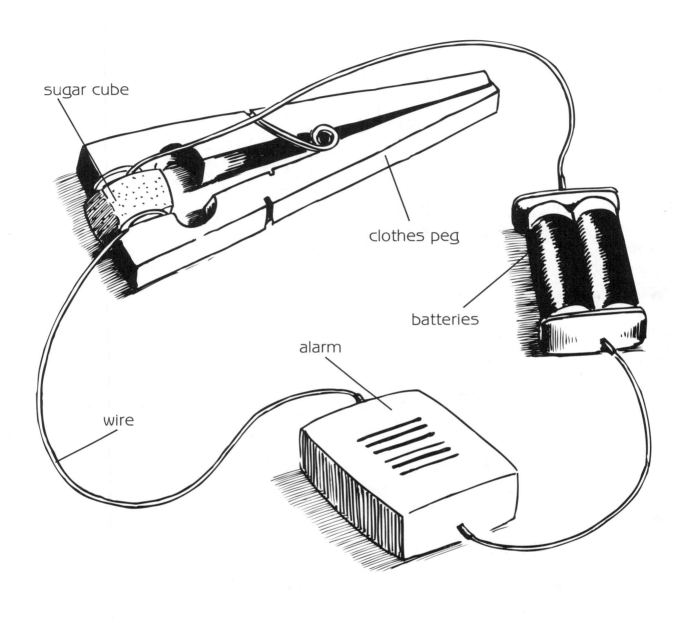

sugar cube

clothes peg

batteries

alarm

wire

_____

_____

_____

_____

_____

_____

Alarming!

● Design and make an alarm for a door being opened

● or a jewellery box being opened

● or a milkman trap.

Things you might need:	wire	drawing pins	battery
alarm	pegs	foil	paper clips	card

ICT

These ICT sheets for Year 4 children cover: cut-and-paste word-processing activities; developing images using colour in-fills (and saving the results); work leading to using branching databases, pie charts and graphs; and using LOGO to manipulate a screen turtle. In all cases children are expected to either use the sheet with appropriate computer software, or to move on to complete an activity using a computer. Clearly, at the heart of ICT lies the computer. It is not a machine to be used as an add-on, an afterthought, or optional convenience gadget. If you use these worksheets without a computer you will not be meeting the requirements of the ICT curriculum.

The QCA scheme for ICT contains five units for Year 4; each unit requires hardware, software and an unspecified amount of time. These sheets focus on activities consistent with aims set down in those units.

Order (page 123)

Objectives: To cut and paste to reorder text; to use font sizes and effects appropriately.

What to do: Clearly this is an exercise to be carried out on the computer. Type in the text for the children to manipulate. They will need to have been shown how to copy, move, cut, paste and generally edit text on the screen. The focus of the sheet is communicating information effectively and efficiently. Children should first consider what are the most important facts. What should be made more prominent by the use of bold or a different font? In what time order should the text be placed? What would be a suitable format for a report of an important official occasion like this?

Differentiation: Let children who have difficulty grasping the concepts involved here cut up the sheet into strips, with each strip containing one aspect of the service. Then they physically rearrange the data and paste it onto a blank sheet of paper. This is the process that they then replicate on the computer.

Extension: Challenge more able children to print out a finished product using such design features as they are able to operate, for example using borders, inserting pictures. You can type up additional text for further practice – rearrange an article from a newspaper, such as a report on a cricket match.

A place for colour (page 124)

Objective: To recognise that ICT can be used to develop images.

What to do: Your children will need access to a suitable computer graphics package such as *Microsoft Paint*, which comes standard with all copies of *Windows*. You may wish to give your children the opportunity to experiment with the package for a time first. Ask them to select a design and then create a repeating pattern such as one finds on wallpaper or wrapping paper. Then, using the design scanned in from the photocopiable sheet, challenge the children to develop the image using colour, in-fill, resizing, different brush sizes and effects. Show them how to copy, save and print, if they do not already know how.

Differentiation: Differentiation will mainly be a matter of allowing the less confident computer-users more time to practise and to complete the computer activity. You may have to accept that some children will not make as much progress as others. More able children will refine and develop images with considerable skill, but all children should be able to use the graphics package to some extent.

Extension: Make a class 'electronic' picture gallery of the most refined images. The design here is in the style of 1920s art nouveau and you may wish to explore other similar designs more fully. For homework children might be asked to find out more. Can they make their own design in his style and scan it into the computer?

Yes or no? (page 125)

Objective: To create a series of yes/no questions to identify objects.

What to do: After identifying the object and writing its name in the space provided, children must then eliminate all the none-yes/no questions from the list given. Discuss the exercise. Which questions would be most useful in discovering what an object is, questions answered *yes* or questions answered *no*? (The more *yes* answers the better.) This task is only an introduction to the use of branching databases. You should progress to creating a tree diagram to identify an object.

Differentiation: In a small group, let the children play a question-and-answer game (*yes* and *no* answers only) to try to identify a hidden object. Adult intervention may be necessary to make sure that questions are framed correctly as there is a tendency to ask 'double' questions, such as *Is it covered in chocolate or marzipan?* (This is really two questions.)

Extension: Have a number of databases (for example on plant, bird or insect identification) on the computer for children to search. Give children a picture of a bird, unnamed, and ask them to use the database to identify it.

Graphs for a purpose (page 126)

Objectives: To learn that different graphs are used for different purposes; to use ICT to create a pie chart.

What to do: Make sure that children understand the instructions on the sheet. The graphs can be named in any suitable way. They contain data on **1.** vehicles travelling on a Sunday; **2.** vehicles travelling on a Monday; **3.** monthly rainfall over a year; **4.** growth of a child over four years. Children should be given credit according to the precision of their titles. In this context long titles are usually more accurate. Children could colour and then cut out the pie charts for comparison. It becomes clearer that there are proportionately more lorries on the road on Monday than Sunday when you can put the relevant segments on top of each other for comparison purposes. Talk about the pie charts and the information displayed. *Why would there be more lorries on Monday than Sunday?* Collecting and graphically presenting the data for the second part of the activity should be straightforward, but it is intended that the pie charts be created using suitable software, such as *Excel.*

Differentiation: It is the first part of the sheet that may pose the most difficulty. You will need to talk through the graphs with the children, identifying the axes on the rain and height graphs, for example. Assistance with using the graphics package should be given by an adult if it is required.

Extension: Pie charts are useful for making comparisons between populations, so give children a suitable hypothesis to test. For example, *Which group has the highest proportion of cyclists in the class, girls or boys? Which group is most interested in swimming, girls or boys?*

Turning turtle (page 127)

Objectives: To recognise that the screen turtle reacts with the same movement that is shown by the line it draws; to use the repeat instruction, predicting what will happen.

What to do: Children will need to be able to operate a screen turtle, and with the size of numbers used and the measurement of turns in degrees. The sheet is straightforward – direct children to compare their prediction with what is actually drawn on the screen by the turtle. They should print out the screen design for comparison. The task is effectively self-marked, unless, of course, the child enters the data incorrectly in the computer. It would be sensible to print out a 'correct' design yourself first to use to check the children's results (they can then check for themselves).

Differentiation: Children will cope with this activity with varying degrees of success. You may find it necessary to go back to using a floor turtle with some children to establish the principles involved.

Extension: Children should progress to writing repeating procedures (such as square, pentagon) and to using these to produce particular effects in more complex designs. (For suggestions see QCA ICT scheme Unit 4E.)

Order

Using your word processor, rearrange the information about the funeral service of Queen Elizabeth the Queen Mother to make it clearer and easier to understand. You can change fonts and sizes and move text around.

(edit text)   (cut and paste)   (re-order)

ORDER OF SERVICE

At the end, the national anthem will be sung.

As the procession leaves the abbey, the organ will play the 'Prelude and Fugue in E flat' by Bach.

Before the service starts the tenor bell of the abbey will toll once every minute for 101 minutes, one toll for every year of Her Majesty the Queen Mother's life.

At 11.30 am on Tuesday 9th April 2002, the procession will enter the Great West Door of Westminster Abbey as the choir sings.

Before the service music will be played. This will include 'Solemn Melody' by Henry Walford Davies and 'Piece d'Orgue', by Bach.

Dr Wesley Carr, Dean of Westminster, will start the service itself by reading a bidding prayer. This will be followed by:

The blessing will be said, after which a trumpeter will sound the 'Last Post' and the service will end.

The first lesson, read by Dr David Hope, Archbishop of York then:
Psalm 121 (sung by the choir).

The second lesson, read by Cardinal Cormac Murphy-O'Connor, Archbishop of Westminster. This will be followed by the first hymn: 'Immortal, invisible God only wise'. Dr George Carey, Archbishop of Canterbury, will deliver the sermon.

The final reading will be from *Pilgrim's Progress*.

Then the choir will sing an anthem 'How lovely are thy dwellings fair'.
Prayers will be followed by the second hymn: 'Guide me, O thou great Redeemer'.

A place for colour

Scan this black and white design into your computer (ask your teacher). Colour the shapes to make an exciting design. Save your work, then print it out.

scan   save as   copy   print

Yes or no?

● This is a _____ .

● Put a tick by all the questions below that can be answered **yes** or **no**.

● If someone could not see the object above, which **yes** or **no** questions would help them to work out what it was? Cut them out and then arrange them in the best order.

How many legs has it got? ☐

Is it made of metal? ☐

How big is it? ☐

Can you pick it up? ☐

Is it used in the house? ☐

What is it made of? ☐

Is it used in the garage? ☐

What room in the house is it used in? ☐

Has it got a handle? ☐

What do we use it for? ☐

Is it used for cooking? ☐

Do we watch it? ☐

Can I turn it on? ☐

Is it big or small? ☐

Do we boil eggs in it? ☐

Do we have one in the classroom? ☐

What colour is it? ☐

What does it taste like? ☐

Can I eat it? ☐

Graphs for a purpose

● These charts and graphs show different data. Give each one a title.

Sunday

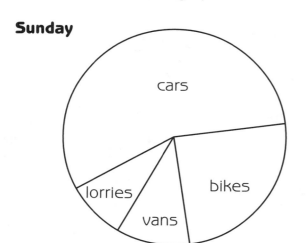

Monday

cars

bikes

lorries

vans

1. _____

_____

2. _____

_____

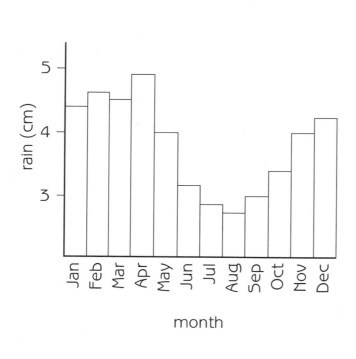

3. _____

_____

4. _____

_____

● Collect data on the number of boys and girls in your **class**. Use ICT to make a pie chart of your data.

● Collect data on the number of boys and girls in your **school**. Use ICT to make a pie chart. What can you learn by comparing the two charts you have made?

Turning turtle

Use the screen turtle (LOGO) to test the following
instructions. Sketch what you think will appear on the screen.

Commands	My prediction
forward 80, right 90, forward 80, left 90, forward 80, right 90, forward 80, left 90, forward 80, right 90, forward 80, left 90, forward 80	
forward 150, right 90, forward 150, right 90, forward 150, right 90, forward 150	
forward 180, right 120, forward 180, right 120, forward 180, right 120	
forward 120, right 90 (repeat four times)	
forward 100, left 6 (repeat six times)	

ART AND DESIGN

Given the wide-ranging aims of the curriculum, the sheets in this section can only be a springboard for further work and experience. Children must not deal with art solely on the scale of A4 so you cannot assume that activities in this section begin and end with a single piece of paper.

Art and design is not just a subject to learn, but an activity that you can practise: with your hands, your eyes, your whole personality. Thus is quoted Quentin Blake in the National Curriculum, a quotation that puts the Key Stage 2 approach to art and design in a nutshell. It is not just a matter of what children have to do, but what they have to experience. Children should, for example, examine and question the work of creative people, whether they are artists, designers, architects or sculptors, so there is clearly plenty of art and design 'fieldwork' for children to do. They should also start to compile a portfolio of their own work; in particular they should build up a record of their observations by using a sketchbook, a record that should follow them through their junior school years.

The QCA scheme suggests a programme that requires between 30 and 36 hours to complete satisfactorily, but this subject is time hungry and teachers may well find that they wish to allocate more. The tasks in this section will help to underpin the approaches suggested in the QCA Scheme of Work. If you wish to study the QCA schemes in more detail they are available at www.standards.dfee.gov.uk/schemes.

Varying viewpoints (page 130)

Objective: To find and record interesting and different viewpoints.

What to do: Make sure that all children have a sketchbook. This should be something that was started in previous years and that remains with the child throughout primary schooling. They should also possess a choice of lead pencils including a soft 2B. Viewfinders should have been constructed and used lower down the school and need to be available for this activity.

The sheet gets the children to focus on different, and in some cases unusual, views of the built environment. They should make a collection of brief sketches of their observations focusing on a particular aspect, for example windows, doors, chimneys, gates and fences, public seating, street furniture and so on. Use the key words on the sheet as triggers for their work – *up*, *down*, *around*, *through*, *underneath* and *reflection*. The illustrations are there for guidance only.

Differentiation: There is no wrong or right response

to this activity so all children should be able to complete the task at their level. If children have difficulty with taking a viewpoint, make sure that the viewfinders are being used properly.

Extension: You may progress from this task to making similar sketches in different lights, at different times of the day and in different weathers. This is therefore a task that might be revisited over a period of time. Children might also add to their sketchbook as a homework activity.

Collograph (page 131)

Objective: To select an image and develop a design for a print.

What to do: A collograph is a card block print and this sheet provides an 'investigating-and-making' activity. You will need to provide the materials and equipment for making a printing block, and the printing ink and rollers to print from it. Use water-based ink that can be cleaned up fairly easily. If you are unfamiliar with the techniques involved you should try it for yourself first. There are many good books on the subject.

Children follow the practical sequence given on the sheet but you should discuss with them (the class or a group) the subject of their work. The idea is that they use a sketch or sketches from their sketchbook as inspiration for their design. This is not a matter of realism but of exploring techniques and conveying ideas.

Differentiation: All children should be able to tackle this activity at their level and differentiation is effectively by outcome. However, this activity can be messy and expensive if children are not properly supervised. Some children may need to be closely monitored throughout.

Extension: Extension is really a matter of giving time and opportunity to explore the technique and to acquire greater technical control. They should try overprinting, the use of several colours, half-drops, full drops, rotations of designs and so on.

Dream art (page 132)

Objective: To develop designs using what they have learned from the study of other artists.

What to do: The sheet provides an example of a photographer's work that fits within the general theme of 'dreams'. You may wish to show children more photographs that have a dream-like quality before they attempt the task. The challenge is to develop a print design inspired by a 'dream' photograph, using the printing skills developed earlier (see previous activity,

'Collograph'). They may modify or improve one of their existing designs, and they should certainly be directed to consider how they might improve or change their design to achieve the quality of print that they want.

Differentiation: Help can be given to those who find this difficult by providing more examples to examine and more opportunity to talk about them. What gives the photographs a dream-like quality? How can we replicate this in some way?

Extension: Getting children to improve or rework their designs is not always easy. It is not something that necessarily comes naturally. It might be advisable to leave this activity and return to it at a later date with the single intention of getting children to rework their print.

Choose a chair (page 133)

Objectives: To explore ideas about chairs; to design one to suit a particular/unusual character.

What to do: The pictures focus children's attention on the range of chairs that are possible. The questions direct their observations. It is a good idea to put children into groups to tackle this sheet. Appoint one 'scribe' who is responsible for recording the group's answers to the questions. The chairs have deliberately not been named. You might challenge the group to identify them.

The 'investigating-and-making' aspect of the sheet requires the provision of materials for the construction of a model chair. You will need to use your judgement here and bear in mind health and safety considerations.

This can be an individual task or a paired activity. The 'unusual' character, for whom the chair is being designed, may be someone currently in the public eye, or a popular cartoon or story character. Let the children use their imagination – for example, Tin Man (Wizard of Oz), Mr Blobby, Iron Man (Ted Hughes).

Differentiation: The intellectual and creative challenge of this work will be reduced if children are given too much direction, but you may wish to differentiate the amount of intervention that you make. For example, you might direct that a particular type of chair be made, a particular character be selected, or that the chair be made to particular measurements.

Extension: Decorate the chair. Children need to make decisions about how to decorate the chair so that it reflects the character of the person that they have chosen. Collect pictures for a 'Chair gallery'. Ask the children to continue the search for homework. Look for chairs from around the world, from different cultures, income groups, made from different materials, in a range of sizes, shapes and so on.

Patterns from journeys: a map
(page 134)

Objectives: To explore how lines and symbols can be used to create patterns; to create a decorative piece of work based upon a real or imagined journey.

What to do: This sheet provides a source that is intended to initiate children's own artwork on the theme of 'journeys'. The provision of art materials has been left broadly open-ended because you may have clear ideas about the medium you wish the children to use. However, the most likely choices will be painting, collage or printing.

First should come observation. Get the class to look closely at the map – it is a work of art in its own right. (You can enlarge this example and use other OS maps as inspiration.) Use the questions on the sheet to focus the discussion. You might wish children to tackle this task in a small group rather than in class discussion. Next direct the children to create a picture using a combination of lines, shapes and colours as well as signs and symbols, on the theme of a journey, using the map for inspiration.

Differentiation: Differentiation will be by the degree of adult intervention. There are no right or wrong answers here. You might find that projecting the image as an OHP transparency emphasises the abstract quality of the map and helps children to grasp the object of the exercise more readily. Limit the choice of medium if necessary.

Extension: Ask children to take an OS map and to sketch individual designs and patterns that they can see from it in their sketchbooks. This might be a task for homework.

Varying viewpoints

● Use your viewfinder in the school grounds to look and find unusual and different viewpoints.

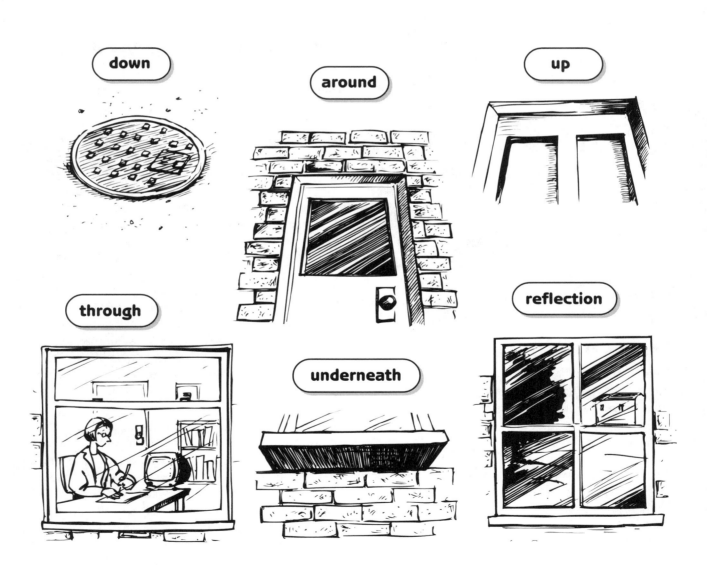

● Sketch each view in your sketchbook.

Collograph

● Use a photo or video image, or a sketch from your sketchbook, to develop your own personal design.

You will need (for the printing block):

strong card
matchsticks
PVA glue
wool
string
textured fabric

You will also need:

printing ink   paint roller   large sheet of plain paper   old magazines

Instructions

● Make your printing block. Form shapes out of different materials and place them onto card. Link and overlap them. Make them touch the edge of the card.

● Now glue the shapes onto your piece of card securely and wait for them to dry.

● Cover the shapes on the card with water-based printing ink using a roller.

● Using the block, print one colour several times onto the large sheet of paper, rubbing into corners with fingertips.

● Remove traces of ink from the card using old magazines.

● Change colour and print a shadow image, slightly to one side of the first image, to create a pleasing design.

Dream art

Study this photograph carefully. It takes you into a dream world. Make a print design called 'Dreams' using ideas suggested by this photograph.

Choose a chair

● Study these chairs.

● Look at the shape and height of the seats and their backrests.
● How are the chairs similar? How are the chairs different?
● How are the chairs used? What is their purpose?
● What are they made of?
● How are they made?

● Design a chair for an unusual character.
● Construct a scale model chair, using cards, tubes or other suitable materials.

Patterns from journeys: a map

- Study the map.
- What are the different lines used for?
- What shapes have been used?
- How are buildings and other objects shown?

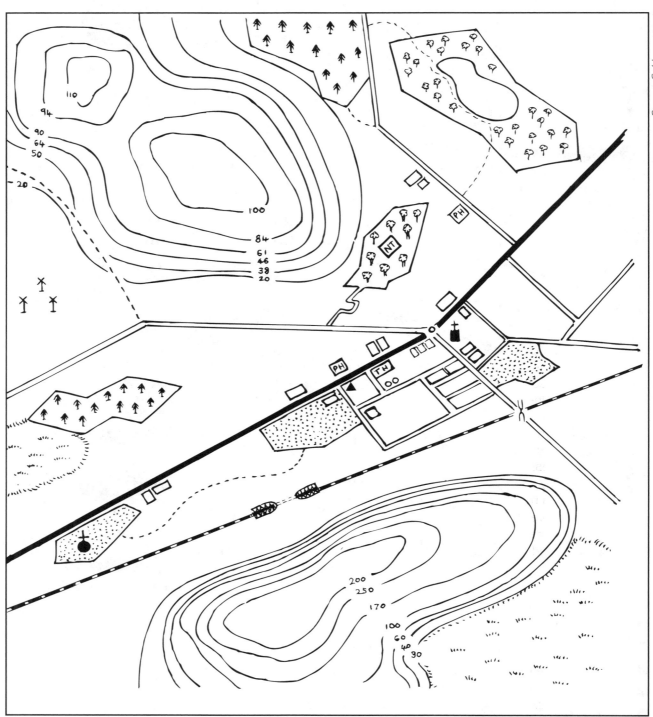

- Make a picture of a journey (it doesn't have to be a real one). Use your own signs and symbols.

MUSIC

The music programme for Year 4 children builds upon the musical experiences of previous years and when you use these sheets you will find that assumptions have been made about prior learning and knowledge. The National Curriculum is progressive and teachers should expect to be able to build upon previous work.

'Listening and performing' are key elements in the Programme of Study and our sheets do make reference to, and suggestions for, these activities, although children will need to move beyond the A4 sheet to carry them out. Musical skills require regular practice. In particular, children are expected to develop the use of their voices, to build up a simple repertoire of songs that they can sing from memory with increasing control and accuracy and to listen carefully. That is the background against which these supporting worksheets should be operating. Singing and music making must be part of a regular, even daily, school experience.

Using the QCA Scheme of Work as a yardstick, we can expect that between 9 and 18 hours be allocated to specific work on music for Year 4, plus a core element of skills reinforcement and practice that would consume around 9 hours – a total year maximum of some 27 hours. It would seem to be an inadequate allocation of time if performance, repetition and practice are taken into account. But music making does occur in small corners of the timetable – at the end of the day, before assembly, in assembly – and this time does accumulate inexorably.

You may feel that specific knowledge or expertise is needed to teach music, and it is true that subject specific skills and knowledge are required increasingly as the child progresses through the school. But this is the same for every subject and at what point one calls in the experts is a matter for debate. You should not be reticent, however, in approaching your music co-ordinator for professional advice and support. You cannot be expected to know everything!

Take five: the pentatonic scale

(page 137)

Objective: To play ostinati based upon the pentatonic scale.

What to do: Provide the five chime bars (or equivalent) as indicated on the sheet and a pair of suitable beaters. Children play the repeating patterns (ostinati), counting the three or four beats in the bar as shown. If they then try this with a friend they can experiment with playing two different ostinati at the same time. Those with the same number of beats in the bar will fit together easily. Because of the particular attributes of the pentatonic scale, any combination of notes from the scale will make a suitable ostinato. When the children write down their own ostinato for the final task, they cannot get it wrong!

Children should use two hands when playing with the beaters and should be shown how to hold them (lightly, bouncily in each hand). The five notes of the pentatonic scale (the first three notes of any major scale plus the fifth and sixth) have particular qualities – any combination of notes can be played without undue tonal clash, and the tunes can sound 'oriental' in texture. The scale used here is the pentatonic scale from the scale of C (CDEGA). You might also like to use the pentatonic scales of G: GABDE or F: FGACD.

Differentiation: Differentiate by the allocation of time and opportunity. You may need facilities that allow a child to practise for some time without disturbing the rest of the class (outside the classroom). Keeping the rhythm going will pose difficulty for some and in this case an adult or competent child could act as conductor and beat/count the beats in the bar.

Extension: Familiarise the class with the scale by singing songs based upon it ('Rain, rain go away', 'Land of the silver birch' and so on). Play the particular pentatonic scale for each song before singing it.

Take five into the forest (page 138)

Objective: To compose a simple melody and accompaniment using the pentatonic scale.

What to do: This uses the pentatonic scale from F. The tune is played using beaters on an instrument (see above 'Take five: the pentatonic scale'). Children make up their own pentatonic song using a seven-note pattern. The accompaniment to the story is meant to be exploratory and children can compose it in groups.

Differentiation: Provide extra supervision and tuition to those who struggle to handle the beaters effectively. You should also provide extra practice time.

Extension: Ask children to work in pairs and to play their compositions together (simultaneously). Discuss the effects. They might also write words to go with their tunes.

Mood music (page 139)

Objective: To create sounds which describe moods or emotions.

What to do: Children can tackle the first two questions by writing their answers directly onto the sheet in the spaces provided. After examining the picture (*Island in the Sound* by Albert Bierstadt), they will need to

record words, or phrases, that they think match the feel of the picture. These could be written on strips of paper to be pinned up on a board alongside the picture as an aide-memoire for their composition. Devising a suitable 'sound picture' can be done individually or as a group. Talk about the activity. Relate colour and texture in art to musical colours.

Differentiation: Less able children (particularly those who might baulk at the written aspect of this sheet) should work in supportive groups. Writing problems should not be allowed to inhibit musical progress.

Extension: Children should listen to music that is strong in mood or emotion – 'Mars' from Holst's *Planet Suite*, for example – and be challenged to describe the mood involved. Ask children to find a piece of music that makes them feel sad. (This is given as an example of a possible homework task.)

Sounds and pictures (page 140)

Objective: To create sounds which paint a picture.

What to do: This sheet is a variation on the activity described in the previous one. However, in this case, the picture tells a story and the music that the children create also needs to have a narrative element in it. The composing aspect should be a co-operative activity.

Differentiation: Differentiate by the allocation of support as suggested in the notes for the previous sheet.

Extension: Repeat the activity using different pictures. Children might link this to their work in art lessons by composing music to go with a picture of their own. The class could play their way through a class picture gallery.

© Corel

Game for a song (1) (page 141)

Objective: To sing and play a range of singing games.

What to do: Introduce this sheet after the class have talked about and explored a range of singing games. Ask them to perform some that they know. Although some are not easily pigeon-holed, try to find some in the categories listed on the sheet (choosing, clapping, skipping, ball, dancing, counting). Some involve more than one of these activities.

Children can describe the game illustrated on the worksheet as directed but they should be given the space and opportunity to play it. This must be a group activity and they will need ample space. Skipping ropes required.

Differentiation: A classroom assistant (ideally one who can skip!) should work with any group of children whose co-ordination lets them down. Skipping will be second nature to some but not to others.

Extension: Have a playground games afternoon. Invite in a few capable parents (or grandparents) to teach and play these games with the children. This can be a good social as well as educational occasion.

Game for a song (2) (page 142)

Objective: To sing and play a range of singing games.

What to do: The instructions on the sheet are straightforward but you will need to play or sing the tune to the class. They should learn it by rote. Divide the class into small groups (at least three in each) and let them devise a game to match the song. Provide balls, skipping ropes and perhaps tambours (or similar) for the children to experiment with.

The words and rhythm point to this being a skipping game but if the children devise a fitting alternative, so be it.

Differentiation: A skipping, clapping, numerate classroom assistant is called for again, preferably one who can also sustain a tune reasonably. Some children will need this support.

Extension: A real challenge is to ask children to devise their own singing game. They will need to make up a short song – four lines are enough. It does not have to make a great deal of sense for many such songs contain nonsense words that are repeated. Children will need to work in groups on this task and might play their tune on a pitched percussion instrument. Some may have the skill to use a more demanding instrument.

Take five: the pentatonic scale

● Use the five chime bars to practise these **ostinati**.

1	2	3	1	2	3	1	2	3	
	●	●		●	●		●	●	
●			●			●			repeat...
C	E	D	C	E	D	C	E	D	

●		●	●		●	●		●	
	●			●			●		repeat...
G	E	A	G	E	A	G	E	A	

1	2	3	4	1	2	3	4	1	2	3	4	
			●				●				●	
		●				●				●		
	●				●				●			
●				●				●				repeat...
C	D	E	G	C	D	E	G	C	D	E	G	

●				●				●				
	●				●				●			
		●				●				●		repeat...
			●				●				●	
G	E	D	C	G	E	D	C	G	E	D	C	

● Play them with a friend. Play two different ostinati at the same time. Which go together best?

● Write an ostinato using *only* these five notes: C, D, E, G, A.

Take five into the forest

Pentatonic tunes are composed using a special five-note scale. Pentatonic tunes have been sung for hundreds of years in many countries over the world. You may think that they sound oriental. A lot of music uses this scale. Here is a pentatonic scale.

● Play this tune using the pentatonic scale.

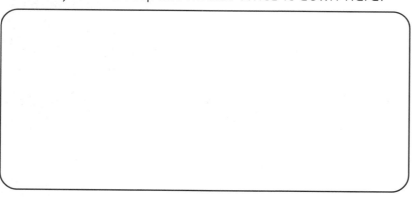

A A F G A D C

● Compose your own tune (use seven notes). Start anywhere! Repeat notes! Write it down here.

● Use the pentatonic scale to accompany this short story. Add drums and percussion with a friend.

The boy entered the dark, dark forest.
The leaves rustled in a gentle breeze.
Suddenly two dogs came crashing through the bushes.
A flock of birds flew up and a cuckoo sang.
The boy turned and ran out of the forest, leaping over stones and clumps of grass.

Mood music

● Music can create different moods and different pictures in the mind. What is your favourite tune? _____

● How does it make you feel? _____

_____

_____

● Look at this picture. Write down as many words and phrases as you can that fit the mood of this picture.

© Corel

● Use instruments to create sounds that match your words and this picture.

■SCHOLASTIC **139**

Sounds and pictures

● Work with a friend. What is happening here? Write down words that describe the picture. List words and phrases that describe how it makes you feel.

● Choose instruments and paint this picture in sound.

© Corel

Game for a song (1)

● With some friends, learn this game.

One, two
Buckle my shoe;
Three, four
Knock at the door;
Five, six
Pick up sticks;
Seven, eight
Lay them straight;
Nine, ten
A big fat hen.

● What kind of game is it? Put a circle round the words that fit.

choosing   clapping   skipping

ball game   dancing   counting

● Play an untuned percussion instrument while the game is being played. Can you play the pulse?

Game for a song (2)

● This is an American singing game. Read the words. Put a circle round the sort of game you think it might be.

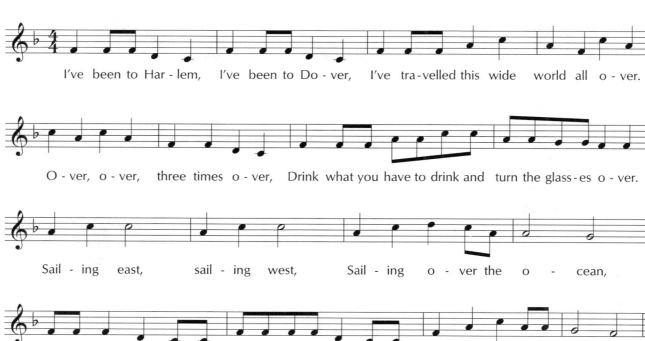

I've been to Har - lem, I've been to Do - ver, I've tra - velled this wide world all o - ver.

O - ver, o - ver, three times o - ver, Drink what you have to drink and turn the glass - es o - ver.

Sail - ing east, sail - ing west, Sail - ing o - ver the o - cean,

Bet - ter watch out when the boat be - gins to rock, or you'll lose your girl in the o - cean.

choosing   clapping   skipping

    ball game   dancing   counting

● Explain your choices.

● Sing the song and play a game that fits it.

RELIGIOUS EDUCATION

The teaching of RE in Year 4 is a *statutory requirement* and must be taught according to a *locally agreed syllabus* in all maintained schools except voluntary-aided and schools of a religious character, where religion should be taught according to a trust deed or guidelines.

Agreed syllabuses tend to share common elements, and the QCA have felt confident enough to produce a scheme of work even though there is no 'national' curriculum around which it might fit. Because religion is closely bound up in strongly held belief, faith communities and cultural heritage, the syllabuses that emerge from the QCA and local SACREs can sometimes sit uneasily with maturation levels of children. In their formulation they have to satisfy many demands, expectations and pressures.

The QCA proposes four study units requiring 24 hours of teaching time. Of course a locally agreed syllabus may not include the same or as many different faiths as are covered by the Year 4 scheme produced by the QCA and so therefore could consume less time. Our sheets cover some of the same ground as this scheme but you can ignore or amend those sheets that do not apply to you.

Where questions about a particular faith community are involved rather than general (generic) information, advice is best sought from members of the faith community themselves.

Aum (page 146)

Objective: To learn and recognise the *aum* symbol and understand its significance to Hindus.

What to do: This is one of those worksheets that should not be given 'cold' to children. Its use has to be set in the context of a study of Hindu worship. The sheet itself contains information which the children need to understand and an activity which should make them familiar with the *aum* symbol and its meaning. Children can draw the aum symbol but might also experiment with and develop ways of writing it more swiftly – with a thick paintbrush, for example.

Looking beyond the symbol, you need to introduce children to the Hindu notion of one god in many forms. Hindus revere and respect the shrines and images of the particular form of god that they choose to worship. Each statue of a *deva* is believed to represent a different attribute of god (just as each child in the class has a different character), but each deity is ultimately a personification of 'Brahman', the ultimate supreme being or god. Hinduism can be regarded as a monotheistic faith that operates as a polytheistic one.

Krishna is one of the ten human appearances of the deity *Vishnu* (one of the three most important deities – the sustainer of life) and is regarded as almost having the status of a deity. *Ganesh*, the elephant-headed god, is revered as the deity who can remove obstacles in the lives of those who worship him.

Differentiation: Differentiation might well be according to cultural background. If you have Hindus in the class, although you should not expect too much from them or pressure them in any way, they could provide useful support for those unfamiliar with the Hindu religion by working in groups alongside them. Videos, books and artefacts (such as a *puja* tray) can also be used to provide background information and support. (Useful sources: Gohil Emporium, 381, Stratford Road, Birmingham B11 4JZ (mail order); www.hindunet.org/god).

Extension: A helpful piece of extension work is to get children to create character portraits of three people, listing their strengths and attributes to get used to the notion of 'gods' having different characteristics. They could be three children, teachers, or people in the public eye. Visit a Hindu temple if you can. Take local advice and plan the visit carefully. Go during *aarti* (a ceremony in which light is offered to the deities), which is usually between 10 and 11am. Check the rules governing behaviour of visitors before you go.

Where is God? A Hindu story
(page 147)

Objective: To reflect upon a Hindu way of expressing belief about the nature of God.

What to do: Children should follow the instructions on the sheet, which are straightforward. The pictures should be rearranged in the following order: **1.** What do you know about God? **2.** Bring salt and water; **3.** Put the salt in the glass; **4.** The next day; **5.** Taste

> Where is the salt?

the water; **6.** God is like that salt. Children need time to discuss and examine this particular Hindu belief; this is best done in a small group. Give the group a particular question to answer or task to tackle. Can they make up a similar story that would explain the Hindu god to somebody? Children from different faith communities may contribute insights from their own understandings of God.

Differentiation: The story is meant to simplify a central tenet of the Hindu faith, so for less able children it is really a case of exemplifying rather than simplifying. Demonstrate the story using salt and water. (Don't drink lots of salt water unless you wish to be sick!) An adult should be on hand to help to stimulate group discussion where this is necessary.

Extension: In order to help children's reflection on the nature of God, they could write poems (*God is…*) or draw or paint pictures to illustrate their idea of God or an aspect of His nature.

How far is it to Bethlehem?

(page 148)

Objective: To understand the significance of Bethlehem to Christians.

What to do: As a prerequisite for doing this sheet, children will need to know the story of Christmas. This is all about locating Bethlehem as a real place existing in the world today. You will need decent atlases for the children to use. Working out the distance from Britain can be done 'as the crow flies' using a ruler or length of string and the scale on a map. (Depending on the children's knowledge, this may require additional instruction.) The story of the journey can be told, written, or illustrated cartoon style.

Differentiation: Some children find maps hard to understand so you should display maps of the area (and a globe), at a decent scale, some time before using the sheet so they can become familiar with the outlines and place names. Instead of calculating the distance, children might access a gazetteer, encyclopedia or approved Internet source to try to find the information.

Extension: Children could annotate the map, perhaps for homework, with information about the Christmas story and/or information about events that have taken place in the area in recent times.

A Christmas carol (page 149)

Objective: To understand how carols and music are used to celebrate the Christmas story.

What to do: Unless the children are particularly competent musicians, you will need to play or sing the carol on the sheet. The tune is 'Here we go round the mulberry bush'. Making up additional verses is not particularly difficult, for example *The shepherds all went to Bethlehem*, or *Jesus was born in Bethlehem* and so on.

Differentiation: It is helpful to sing and clap the song and children may find it easier to make up verses this way. Form a small group, sing the verse that is written, then get children to make up a verse in turn (singing it) that everybody repeats and sings. This way you will build up a series of verses that tell the Christmas story.

Extension: A complete carol can be composed to tell the full story. The children could illustrate it and produce a 'carol sheet' for a Christmas concert. The carol can easily be performed, accompanied on the piano with percussion added. It is also excellent sung *a cappella* (unaccompanied).

The Easter story (1): Palm Sunday (page 150)

Objective: To learn the story of Palm Sunday.

What to do: You will need to provide a diary or calendar that shows the date of Palm Sunday. You will also need bibles that the children can use. It is best to have a few different translations, not just a children's bible (the *Authorised (King James) Version*, *The Good News Bible*, *Revised Standard* and so on). Children will enjoy comparing versions, spotting differences and teasing out meanings of strange words. Ideally you should use this photocopiable sheet during the weeks leading up to Easter.

Differentiation: This work demands high literacy skills so it will be beneficial for some to work in mixed-ability groups. You might also wish to read or tell the story to the class yourself first (perhaps some time before using the sheet) to introduce the story. A local vicar might be willing to contribute to the lesson and show children a sample palm cross, for example.

Extension: Challenge children to expand the cartoon story from four to six pictures (cut out the pictures).

They should add pictures and text where they think best and reconstruct the story by reassembling the cartoon on a large sheet of paper or in a book.

The Easter story (2): the Last Supper (page 151)

Objective: To know the story of the Last Supper and what the Eucharist is.

What to do: There are various approaches to using this sheet, largely dependent upon the level of knowledge of your class. You might wish to use the picture as a focus for class discussion (You can photo-enlarge or create an OHP transparency). *Who are the people here? What are they doing? Can you name any? What do you think happened next?* And so on. Let children read the story themselves and/or read the story to them. Do not spoon-feed children too much, even if they initially know little of the story. Let them try to work out what is going on in the picture. One of the best ways of tackling the latter part of the sheet is not to do it yourself but to let a practising Christian explain the Eucharist. A visit to a church under the direction of the local incumbent is ideal. Try exploring www.culham.ac.uk or www.stapleford-centre.org for teaching ideas.

Differentiation: Limit the less able children to describing what they see in the picture – a simple listing of observations will suffice. More able children should be capable of retelling the story of the Last Supper unaided. Make sure suitable Bibles and books are on hand for reference purposes.

Extension: In John's Gospel, instead of the story of bread and wine is the story of Jesus washing his disciples' feet. Get children to tell this story. What lesson was Jesus trying to teach his disciples?

The Easter story (3) (page 152)

Objective: To learn the main events of the story of the crucifixion and resurrection.

What to do: The matching of pictures and words can only really be done effectively if all the text boxes and pictures are cut out and rearranged. The cartoons tell the outline story of the crucifixion and resurrection but you can fill out as much detail as you feel appropriate to the age and abilities of your children. If children are unfamiliar with the story then they will need to be told it, and you will also need to provide story books and children's Bibles for them to refer to. Other than learning the events of Easter, children need to begin to understand why Christians believe that there is life after death and the symbolism of the cross. This is best done in class discussion.

Differentiation: For many children, coping with the events of the story will be difficult enough without tackling the Christian beliefs that it has given rise to. You may wish to go no further with these children. However, where possible you should go beyond the story to the importance of Easter to Christians even if this is done in the most simplistic way. The journey from fact to belief is a difficult one at whatever level it is attempted, but Christians believe Christ's death and resurrection represent the ultimate triumph of good over evil and the proof that death is not the end but a new beginning.

Extension: Almost any of the pictures illustrating aspects of the story can be used as the focus for more intensive discussion. *Why did Judas betray Jesus? What is betrayal? Why were Jesus's followers afraid when they saw the tomb empty? Why did Pilate wash his hands of Jesus? Why did the Romans want to put Jesus to death?* Choose one question and get children to try to answer it.

Aum

The Hindu symbol for God is **aum**. This is what it looks like:

It is pronounced 'om' and sometimes written that way. The symbol is sacred and so is the sound 'om'. The symbol appears in Hindu homes and places of worship. The sound is used to start and end Hindu prayers.

● Copy the **aum** symbol here.

● Hindus believe there is one God but that there are different images of him. Find out about Ganesh and Krishna.

Where is God? A Hindu story

This story illustrates a Hindu belief about God.
Cut out the pictures and arrange them in the correct order for the story
to make sense.

How far is it to Bethlehem?

● Find Bethlehem on this map. Then find Bethlehem in an atlas. Work out how far away it is from where you live.

● Why is Bethlehem important to Christians?

_____

_____

● Tell the story of a journey to Bethlehem by one of the following:

(Mary and Joseph)   (the wise men)   (the shepherds)

A Christmas carol

Christians sing songs about the birth of Jesus. These are called **carols**.

Here we go up to Beth - le - hem, Beth - le - hem, Beth - le - hem.

Here we go up to Beth - le - hem on a cold and frost - ty morn - ing.

Words © Stainer and Bell

We've got to be taxed in Bethlehem,
Bethlehem, Bethlehem,
We've got to be taxed in Bethlehem
On a cold and frosty morning.

Sydney Carter

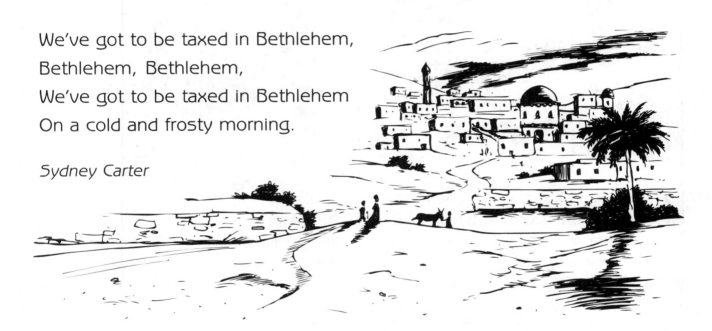

● Write a verse of your own to this tune (it's from 'Here we go round the Mulberry Bush'), telling another part of the Christmas story.

The Easter story (1): Palm Sunday

● Find out when **Palm Sunday** is (look in a diary).

● Why do Christians call it Palm Sunday?

● Read the story here and then compare with the one in the Bible (Matthew 21:1–11).

● Churches often give out **palm crosses** on Palm Sunday. Can you make one?

1. Jesus and his disciples approached the city of Jerusalem. At Bethany, Jesus sent two of his disciples ahead to fetch a donkey.

2. They brought the donkey and laid their cloaks on its back for Jesus to ride.

3. Along the route crowds gathered. They laid cloaks and palm branches in front of the donkey.

4. When Jesus entered Jerusalem, the crowd went wild with excitement. "Who is this?" some people asked. "It is the prophet Jesus from Nazareth," shouted the crowd.

The Easter story (2): the Last Supper

● This is a painting of the last meal Jesus ate with his disciples. You can read the story for yourself (Mark 14:12–26). Describe what is happening in this picture.

The Last Supper (oil on panel) by German School (16th century), Wilanow Palace, Warsaw, Poland/Bridgeman Art Library

● Because they ate bread and drank wine with Jesus, Christians do the same today in the **Eucharist**. Find out all you can about the Eucharist.

The Easter story (3)

This cartoon tells the Easter story. First cut out the pictures and arrange them in the correct order. Then cut out and match the correct words to the pictures.

Judas betrays Jesus with a kiss in the Garden of Gethsemane.	Jesus is crucified with the two bandits at Golgotha.
The High Priest asks Jesus whether he is the Messiah. "I am," he replies.	Jesus is placed in a rock tomb sealed by a huge stone.
Pilate, the Roman governor, can find no harm in Jesus. To satisfy the crowd, he condemns Jesus to be crucified.	On the third day his followers find the tomb empty. They are afraid.

PSHE AND CITIZENSHIP

You are reminded that PSHE and citizenship are not National Curriculum subjects for KS1 and KS2 (citizenship is a statutory requirement at KS3 and KS4). Schools are, nevertheless, expected to promote a child's spiritual, moral, social and cultural development, across the National Curriculum, at all Key Stages.

The knowledge, skills and understanding identified in the *non-statutory framework* for PSHE and citizenship (KS1 and KS2) is to be taught under the following headings: 'Developing confidence and responsibility and making the most of their abilities'; 'Preparing to play an active role as citizens'; 'Developing a healthy, safer lifestyle'; 'Developing good relationships and respecting differences between people'. But because of the non-statutory nature of this framework and the concomitant lack of content prescription, there are many varied ways of teaching to these headings. PSHE is a vast subject and when you add in citizenship, the teaching demands become somewhat overwhelming. Fortunately much of the content readily connects with other subjects in the curriculum. The photocopiable sheets in this section can be used to support approaches to the subject that fit within the National Curriculum framework.

Rules and laws protect us (1)

(page 155)

Objective: To understand that rules and laws are designed to protect us.

What to do: When children describe the law being broken, they can do this in general terms. It is the principle that we are after here, not the identification of a specific Act of Parliament. The first picture shows a road traffic offence (a car speeding in a 30 mph-limit zone); the second shows property theft; and the third an act of violence against another person/thing. The answers the children give to the *how?* question should embody common-sense principles. When you come to discussing their answers, if there are any children who have difficulty understanding why particular acts are wrong and why we need laws to protect us, then put the inverse scenario to the class. *What would happen if there were no traffic laws, no protection against theft, no protection against violence?*

Differentiation: Although some children may need help in interpreting the pictures (this is best done in a small group), the main differentiation here will be by outcome. You should accept brief, even one-word answers here, as long as it is clear what the child's answer is.

Extension: Get children to reflect upon the principles involved. *What would happen if...?* Ask them to draw

pictures, or describe in some other form what might happen if one of the laws discussed was abolished. This could be a homework task.

Rules and laws protect us (2)

(page 156)

Objective: To understand that rules and laws are designed to protect us.

What to do: This is the same as the previous activity, except that these are rules, or conventions in and around the school, not laws of the land. The pictures illustrate running in a confined space; leaving school without permission; and an act of bullying. Get the children to think in terms of 'good practice'. *Would it be good practice for everybody to run about the school? Why not?* Make the point that although these rules are needed to protect the weak and vulnerable, they are needed to protect the strong, too.

Differentiation: Once again, differentiation will be by outcome in the main. It may be necessary to discuss the pictures as a group or as a class (you can make an OHP transparency for projection), especially if you have children who have an underdeveloped sense of morality or are immature socially.

Extension: This is a good opportunity to examine the rules that govern the behaviour of pupils in school. Get the children to choose a rule that they would change or one that they would add to the list of school rules. Make sure that they can explain their choices. Another extension route would be to look at a particular activity or rule that is giving concern in the school. Is bullying a problem? What do they think should be done about it?

Community connections (page 157)

Objective: To be aware of the variety of communities to which we belong simultaneously.

What to do: Define the term *community*, in a simple way, as a group. It has become a loaded, even a pejorative term, often banded about by politicians, so you need to keep the definition simple. However, community usually implies bonds of unity that involve responsibilities, mutual concerns, sometimes rules to govern behaviour and always an element of caring about other members in that community. The interconnected ring on the photocopiable sheet gives the generic names of communities to which the children will belong. They are required to fill in the precise name of that community, for example family name. They should then fill in the blank link with the name of another community they belong to. It is assumed that the latter group will be a larger, global group, hence the hint in the picture of the globe. It could be Great Britain (as opposed to Wales), Europe, the United Nations, the world and so on. The centre of the ring has been left empty for the children. They could draw a portrait or insert a photograph of themselves at the centre of their world.

Differentiation: To stress the interconnectedness of communities, cut out the links before the children complete the naming exercise; they can then piece the ring together and add the picture of themselves at the centre. More able children might well think of additional communities to add (religious, ethnic, and so on).

Extension: Take one of the 'communities' and examine it more closely. Ask children to find out six (or other number) facts about it. For example, how much do they know about their county or the United Nations? This could be research for homework.

Heroes and heroines (page 158)

Objective: To recognise and explore feelings about some role models for young people.

What to do: This activity could become trivialised if the issues are not discussed first. What do we mean by admirable qualities? Distinguish between a quality such as 'loyalty', which involves admirable action on the part of the individual, and a quality such as 'being tall', which does not. Children put the names of their chosen individuals in each of the frames provided. The frames are intended to hold photographs of the children's heroes. This sheet is obviously part of a discussion activity that should be carried out by the whole class. The focus of the discussion can be directed by you to some extent, but as it is an open discussion you need to be prepared for *X is a footballing hero but he takes drugs, assaults his wife, gets into drunken brawls* and so on. Moral issues are not always easy to deal with. X may be a despicable human being but still a brilliant footballer. Should he be a hero? The idea is to let children explore their feelings about issues like this.

Differentiation: Some children (perhaps all) will need preparation for this activity. Ask them to collect pictures of people they regard as their heroes over a period of time – say a week. You could suggest categories that they could choose a hero from, such as the world of sport, or TV. It would be helpful to have support in the form of reference books (an up-to-date child's *Who's who?* would be excellent) to assist them in finding out about their heroes.

Extension: Make a class gallery of 'Heroes and Heroines'. Alongside this you could have a 'Rogues Gallery'. Children might collect pictures as part of a homework task.

In other people's shoes (page 159)

Objective: To be able to put themselves into someone else's shoes.

What to do: This is self-explanatory, but not as easy as it looks. Really seeing the world from somebody else's point of view takes some imagination. Dad's life may seem very easy from the child's viewpoint because they may not have considered (or know about) all the responsibilities and stresses of his life. This sheet is a chance for the children to think about these things. It must be followed up by class discussion.

Differentiation: Encourage the children to discuss the sheet by allowing them to work at this in small groups or in pairs. If writing down their views is a problem, then you should accept answers in note form.

Extension: You might wish to follow up the examination of the role of parents by getting children to list the three (or more) main activities undertaken by them in a specific week. Alternatively you could repeat the activity using different people. For example, examine what it is like to be a police officer, a teacher, a refuse collector, a plumber's mate.

What we do for each other

(page 160)

Objectives: To develop a concern for other people; to appreciate the importance of taking responsibility for themselves and their behaviour.

What to do: The only part of this sheet that might cause concern is the latter part. You need to make sure that children choose, or have chosen for them, a suitable subject. The most obvious choice is a member of the family (mum is illustrated) but this might not be applicable in some cases, which is why the name has been left blank on the sheet. This is not a competition to see who does the most – it is an exercise to draw children's attention to the fact that we all depend upon each other. They may not be aware of the affective side of things, for example they may note that mum makes their sandwiches, but not that she comforts them when they are distressed, gives them love, pays attention to what they say, cares about what they do and so on.

Differentiation: Children can simply list the actions in the spaces provided, although expect more able children to write coherent sentences. Let less able children work in pairs or co-operative groups as you feel is appropriate.

Extension: You could move on to explore 'What would happen if…?' situations. *What would happen if my teacher did not care whether I did my work? If nobody cared whether I came home from school? If nobody cared whether my clothes were dirty?* Choose your focus with care and sensitivity.

Rules and laws protect us (1)

● What laws or rules are being broken in the pictures?
● Explain how the law or rule protects everyone.

Law being broken

_____

_____

How this law protects us

_____

_____

_____

_____

Law being broken

_____

_____

How this law protects us

_____

_____

_____

_____

Law being broken

_____

_____

How this law protects us

_____

_____

_____

_____

_____

Rules and laws protect us (2)

● Which school rules are being broken in these pictures?
● Explain how the rule protects everyone.

Rule being broken

_____

_____

How this rule protects us

_____

_____

_____

_____

Rule being broken

_____

_____

How this rule protects us

_____

_____

_____

_____

Rule being broken

_____

_____

How this rule protects us

_____

_____

_____

_____

Community connections

● Do you know the names of all the communities that you belong to?
Write their names in the right links.

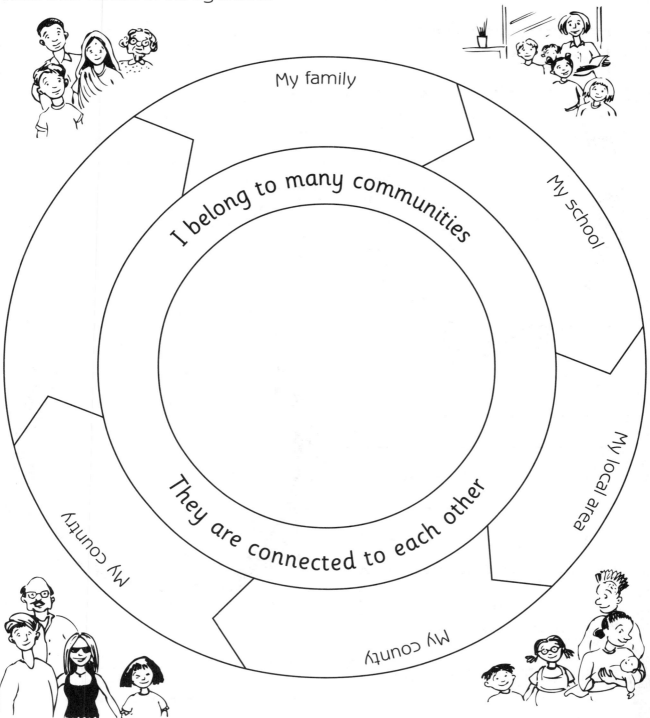

My family

My school

I belong to many communities

They are connected to each other

My local area

My country

My county

● Can you think of another community that you
belong to? Write it in the blank link.

Heroes and heroines

● Who are your heroes or heroines? Draw their portraits in these frames.
● Why do you admire them? What don't you admire about them?

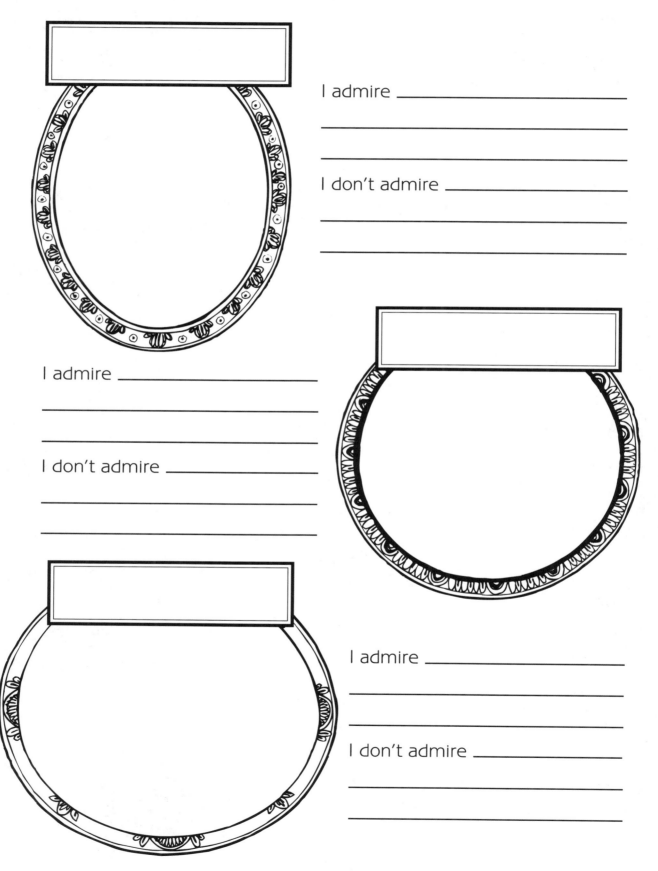

I admire _____

_____

_____

I don't admire _____

_____

_____

I admire _____

_____

_____

I don't admire _____

_____

_____

I admire _____

_____

_____

I don't admire _____

_____

_____

In other people's shoes

The good things about being a dad	The hard things about being a dad

The good things about being a mum	The hard things about being a mum

What we do for each other

What I do to help

at home _____

_____

_____

_____

_____

at school _____

_____

_____

_____

_____

What _____ at home does for me

_____

_____

_____

_____